VILLAGE SWARAJ

VILLAGE SWARAJ

BY
M. K. GANDHI

Compiled by
H. M. VYAS

NAVAJIVAN PUBLISHING HOUSE
AHMEDABAD-14

Rupees Thirty-five

© Navajivan Trust, 1962

First Edition, 5,000 Copies, December, 1962
Second Revised Edition, 10,000 Copies, May, 1963
This Reprint, 2,000 Copies, January, 1996
Total : 17,000 Copies

ISBN 81-7229-140-X

Printed and Published by
Jitendra T. Desai
Navajivan Mudranalaya,
Ahmedabad-380 014 (INDIA)

FOREWORD

It is, indeed, a matter for gratification that the Navajivan Trust is publishing selections from Mahatma Gandhi's writings on "Village Swaraj" in a book form. The publication contains Gandhiji's views on different aspects of rural life including agriculture, village industry, animal husbandry, transport, basic education, health and hygiene. At a time when we are endeavouring to establish Panchayati Raj in India on the basis of wide decentralization of political and economic power, this book is bound to be of great value to a large number of official as well as non-official workers. The Community Development movement should not be regarded as some kind of a programme which has been largely imported from the Western democracies; it must necessarily be based on Indian conditions and traditions. It is, therefore, of paramount importance that all workers who are being trained for participating in this movement should possess ample knowledge about Gandhiji's ideas in regard to various aspects of rural reconstruction. If we overlook and bypass Gandhiji's experience and ideals about the pattern of Indian planning, we shall be doing so at great peril to the evolution of our democracy on sound foundations.

It is wrong to think that Gandhiji entertained outmoded ideas regarding modern Industrialization. As a matter of fact, he was not against mechanization as such; he strongly objected to "the *craze* for machinery". He welcomed every improvement in small machines which could provide employment to millions of artisans in the villages. In place of mass production by big factories he advocated production by the masses in their own homes and cottages. Gandhiji was most anxious to provide full employment to every able-bodied citizen of India, and he maintained that this objective could be achieved only by organizing village and cottage industries in the countryside in an efficient manner. Any economic planning which did not utilize fully the idle manpower in the rural areas could not be termed as sound or rational. "To a people, famishing and idle," said Gandhiji, "the only acceptable form in which God can dare appear is work and promise of food as wages." (*Selections from Gandhi*, by N. K. Bose, p. 49) This ideal of full employment is now recognized by Western economists as basic to planned economic development, particularly of underdeveloped countries with large and growing populations. Prof. Galbraith is of the view that "full employment is more desirable than increased production combined with unemployment". (*The Affluent Society*, p. 155)

Mahatma Gandhi strongly pleaded for decentralization of economic and political power through the organization of Village Panchayats. He was of the definite view that Panchayat system in India, if worked on scientific lines, could not only build up the social and economic strength of the countryside but also strengthen the forces of national defence against the risk of foreign invasion. Acharya Vinoba Bhave has also been laying great stress on the urgent need for organizing the Indian villages on a co-operative community basis through *Gramadana*. This ideal of decentralized democracy or Panchayati Raj should not be regarded as a sentimental proposition based on medieval notions. A study of modern economic and political thought in the

West would indicate that decentralized institutions are now regarded as crucial to the establishment of democracy on stable foundations. "If man's faith in social action is to be revivified," states Prof. Joad, "the State must be cut up and its functions distributed." (*Modern Political Theory*, pp. 120-21) In his *Fabian Socialism*, Prof. Cole maintains that for diffusing widely among ordinary men and women a capacity for collective activity "we must set out to build our society upon little democracies". From this standpoint, the experiment of Panchayati Raj which has been launched in India's countryside with zeal and vigour is a right step towards the goal of "Village Swaraj" envisaged by Gandhiji.

Above all, we should be clear in our minds that Gandhiji did not stand for a social and economic order based on material values alone. He always upheld the ideal of plain living and high thinking and worked for a higher *standard of life* and not merely for a higher *standard of living*. "Civilization, in the real sense of the term", remarks Gandhiji, "consists not in the multiplication but in the deliberate and voluntary restriction of wants."

Unfortunately, this ethical and moral aspect of economic life has often been neglected to the detriment of real human welfare. Modern economists are now emphasizing the urgent need for 'investment in man' in addition to 'investment in goods' for achieving broad-based and speedy economic growth. Prof. Schumpeter rightly observes that for the success of economic and political democracy, "individuals with adequate ability and moral character must exist in sufficient numbers". (*Capitalism, Socialism and Democracy*) The same idea has been forcefully expressed by Mr. Crosland in the following words: "We do not want to enter the age of abundance only to find that we have lost the values which might teach us how to enjoy it." (*Future of Socialism*, p. 529) It is, therefore, this human and moral aspect of our planning which must be constantly borne in mind by all workers, officials as well as non-officials, who are engaged in this great adventure of building up a New India of Gandhiji's dreams.

New Delhi
13-11-1962

                              SHRIMAN NARAYAN

PREFACE

Never before in history did the ideal of human unity attract so much attention of world statesmen and scientists, literary men and laymen alike as it does today. In the words of Shri Aurobindo, "Today the ideal of human unity is more or less vaguely making its way to the front of our consciousness. The intellectual and material circumstances of the age have prepared and almost imposed upon it, especially the scientific discoveries which have made our earth so small that its vastest kingdoms seem now no more than the provinces of a single country."* Arnold Toynbee observes rightly, "The West's prowess in technology has, as we put it poetically, 'annihilated distance' and has at the same time armed human hands, for the first time in history with weapons capable of annihilating the humane race. . . . The reason why we need unity so urgently now is both sensational and commonplace. It has been put curtly in the epigram 'one world or none'. It is obvious to every politically conscious man and woman in the world today that in the Atomic Age if we do not now abolish war, war is going to abolish us."† Pitirim Sorokin has in his inimitable language put the present problem that faces the world thus: "Bleeding from war wounds and frightened by the atomic Frankensteins of destruction, humanity is desperately looking for a way out of the

---

* *The Ideal of Human Unity.*

† *One World and India.* All quotations of Toynbee are from this book.

deathtrap. It craves life instead of inglorious death.
It wants peace in place of war. It is hungry for love in
lieu of hate. It aspires for order to replace disorder.
It dreams of a better humanity, of greater wisdom,
of a finer cultural mantle for its body than the bloody
rags of its robot civilization. Having foolishly
manoeuvred itself into a deathtrap and facing the in-
exorable problem, 'To be or not to be', it is forced to
pursue, more desperately than ever before, its eternal quest for survival and immortality."*

If humanity that is now challenged by death-
dealing weapons fails to act in time on right lines the
alternative is total destruction. The saving of mankind lies in the establishment of World Government.
The necessity of abolishing war makes it inevitable.
The establishment of a genuine World Government
necessarily involves the abolition of the national
sovereignty of the existing States.

How the World Government will be established
is an important question as the shedding of national
sovereignty will not be easy to achieve. There will be
but very few politicians who would say like
Gandhiji: "I see nothing grand or impossible about
our expressing our readiness for universal inter-
dependence rather than independence. . . . The logical sequel of self-sacrifice is that the individual sacrifices himself for the community, the community for
the district, the district for the province, the province for the nation, and the nation for the world."
Arnold Toynbee observes, "In the Atomic Age, the
spirit that we need in our statesmen is surely Ashoka's
spirit (i.e. non-violence). We can no longer do without
unity. But we can also no longer afford to pursue this

Reconstruction of Humanity.

indispensable objective by methods of coercion. Conversion not coercion, is in our day, the only means that we can employ for unity of mankind. In the Atomic Age, the use of force would result not in union, but in self-destruction. In this age, fear, as well as conscience, commands a policy that Ashoka in his time, was inspired to follow by conscience alone." It is thus clear that the way of violence is closed to humanity for all time. Mahatma Gandhi observed in his Foreword to Shri Bharatan Kumarappa's *Villagism*: "The past two wars of our generation have proved the utter bankruptcy of such economic orders. Incidentally, the wars seem to me to have proved the bankruptcy of war." May we say that it is now the Age of Non-violence that has set in! The world will have no alternative but to tap this inexhaustible treasure of non-violence which hitherto was looked upon as if in contempt by all-wise politicians of the world. Gandhiji believed that India had a definite mission to fulfil. He says: "An India awakened and free has a message of peace and good-will to a groaning world." Another time he said, "I feel in the innermost recesses of my heart. . . that the world is sick unto death of blood-spilling. The world is seeking a way out, and I flatter myself with the belief that perhaps it will be the privilege of the ancient land of India to show the way out to the hungering world." According to Arnold Toynbee "India's special contribution will have been her large-heartedness and broad-mindedness. . . . and this, I believe, is going to be recognized by future generations, in retrospect as having been India's characteristic gift to a united human race."

Establishment of world peace through World

Government will remain an empty dream so long as the ultimate sanction for resolving disputes remains military force. Use of force must be completely ruled out if we want permanent peace. It is only the World Government backed by a moral sanction that can ensure lasting peace. A world federation based on equality and fraternity of all component units, big or small, would go a long way in the direction of securing world peace. A World Government by itself cannot guarantee peace. For roots of war lie in the conflict-breeding socio-economic systems of the nations. Unless they are transformed from the root, the hope of world peace would be a chimera. A world organization, therefore, should ensure the working of real democracy and elimination of exploitation in every shape or form. It is only the small units which help the working of real democracy and provide a field for the full growth of individuals. The larger the units, the lesser the scope for individual initiative and freedom. Larger organizations tend to curb the individuals and smaller groups as they would work for uniformity and regimentation. They ultimately result in increasing stagnancy and decay. Therefore, it is imperative that for achieving lasting world peace, the present political and economic systems be re-orientated so as to build small decentralized units. Else, the very object of world peace will be frustrated and the World Government will be imperilled bringing in its train vast insurmountable problems. The inevitable choice, therefore, is decentralized political and economic units.

The experience of mankind testifies to the fact that collective life is more genial, varied and fruitful when it is concentrated in small units and simpler organizations. It is only small units which have had the most intense life. Collective life diffusing itself in vast areas would be wanting in cohesiveness and productiveness.

Ancient Greek City States and Village Republics of India provided specimens of all-round development of rich and puissant life.

Pandit Jawaharlal Nehru wrote:

"This system of village self-government was the foundation of the Aryan polity. It was this that gave it strength. So jealous were the village assemblies of their liberties that it was laid down that no soldier was to enter a village except with a royal permit. The *Nitisara* says that when the subjects complain of an officer the king 'should take the side not of his officers but of his subjects'; and if many people complain the officer was to be dismissed, 'for', says the *Nitisara*, 'who does not get intoxicated by drinking of the vanity of office?' Wise words which seem to apply especially to the crowds of officials who misbehave and misgovern us in this country today!

"As late as 1830 a British Governor in India, Sir Charles Metcalfe, described the village communities as follows:

'The village communities are little republics having nearly everything they want within themselves and almost independent of foreign relations. They seem to last where nothing else lasts. This union of the village communities, each one forming a separate little State in itself . . . is in a high degree conducive to their happiness, and to the enjoyment of a great portion of freedom and independence.'

"This description is very complimentary to the old village system. We have a picture of an almost idyllic state of affairs. Undoubtedly, the great deal of local freedom and independence that the villages had was a good thing, and

there were other good features also. . . . The work of
rebuilding and rebirth (of Village Republics) still remains
to be done by us."*

The picture of Village Swaraj as conceived by
Gandhiji is not the resurrection of the old village
Panchayats but the fresh formation of independent
village units of Swaraj in the context of the present-
day world. Village Swaraj is the practical embodiment of non-violence in the spheres of politics, economics and sociology.

According to Gandhiji, ideal society is a Stateless
democracy, the state of enlightened anarchy where
social life has become so perfect that it is self-regu-
lated. "In the ideal state, there is no political power
because there is no State." Gandhiji believed that perfect realization of an ideal is impossible. However
"the ideal is like Euclid's line that is one without
breadth but no one has so far been able to draw it
and never will. All the same it is only by keeping the
ideal line in mind that we have made progress in geometry." In the political field he gave us Village Swaraj nearing the conception of his ideal of Stateless
Democracy. He considers that Government best which
governs the least. According to the communist philosophy, the final phase is the "withering away of the
State". But in the totalitarian State of Russia there
is concentration of all power in the State. It is difficult
to believe that at any time the State there will wither
away. Mahatma Gandhi being a practical idealist,
realized the practical usefulness of the ideal of Stateless Democracy, and presented Village Swaraj which
is not the "withering away of the State" but "scattering of the State". Thus, Village Swaraj is the ideal

*Glimpses of World History.

given expression to on a realizable plane unl
distant goal of the "withering away of the State".

Modern democracies are election-centred,
party-dominated, power-aimed, centralized complicated mechanisms. Concentration of authority
marks almost all present political systems which
have become unwieldy and top-heavy, be they
capitalist, socialist or communist systems. The individuals count no more though as voters they are styled
as masters. They present themselves at periodical elec-
tions for casting votes and then sleep away until the
next one. This is the only political action the individual performs once in a stipulated period. That he
is driven to do under the directions of a centralized party
system, and guidance of the newspapers which
are mainly tools of the centralized economic powers.
The individual has little or no voice in the shaping
of the policy of the government. In a welfare State
or totalitarian regime he is reduced to the position of
a well-fed, dumb, driven animal in human form.

Gandhiji wanted true democracy to function in
India. He, therefore, observed: " True democracy
cannot be worked by twenty men sitting at the centre.
It has to be worked from below by the people of every
village." In Village Swaraj, the village being the
decentralized small political unit endowed with
fullest powers, every individual will have a direct
voice in the government. The individual is the
architect of his own government. The government of
the village will be conducted by a Panchayat of five
persons annually elected by adult villagers possessing minimum prescribed qualifications. It will
have all the authority and jurisdiction. The Panchayat will be the legislature, judiciary and executive

rolled into one as there will be no system of punish-
ment in it.

In such a system of government there will be
citizens who are self-controlled, not authority-control-
led; endowed with initiative and highly developed
sense of civic responsibility in place of those who look
to government for all things.

Real Democracy, i. e. Swaraj works for the full
freedom and growth of the individual who is the
ultimate motive power of a real political system.

Village Swaraj as conceived by Gandhiji is
thus a genuine and virile democracy which offers
a potent cure for many of the political ills that mark
the present political systems. Such a pattern of decentralized genuine democracy will have a message for
the whole of humanity.

To Gandhiji political power was not an end in
itself, but one of the means for enabling people to
better their condition in every sphere of life. He,
therefore, observed in his famous "Last Will and
Testament" that though India has attained political
independence, she " has still to attain social, moral
and economic independence, in terms of seven hundred thousand villages as distinguished from the cities
and towns." It embodied a picture and a programme
of Village Swaraj that is Panchayat Raj which in
other terms is a non-violent self-sufficient, economic
unit with fullest political power. The Village Swaraj
as conceived by Gandhiji is man-centred unlike the
Western economy which is wealth-centred. The
former is the life economy the latter is the death
economy.

Laying down the duties of the village worker
who naturally occupies the pivotal position in the

planning of Village Swaraj of Gandhiji's conception, he says that the village worker will organize the villages so as to make them self-contained and self-supporting through agriculture and handicrafts, will educate the village folk in sanitation and hygiene and will take all measures to prevent ill-health and disease among them and will organize the education of the village folk from birth to death along the lines of Nai Talim.

The politicians of the world who aspire for world peace would think of attempting to plan from top to bottom whereas Gandhiji proposed to work from bottom upwards. He, therefore, says, " Independence must begin at the bottom. Thus every village will be a Republic or Panchayat having full powers. It follows therefore, that every village has to be self-sustained and capable of managing its affairs even to the extent of defending itself against the whole world. It will be trained and prepared to perish in the attempt to defend itself against any onslaught from without. Thus ultimately it is the individual who is the unit." To Gandhiji " self-government means continuous effort to be independent of government control whether it is foreign government or whether it is national. Swaraj government will be a sorry affair if people look up to it for the regulation of every detail of life. " In Village Swaraj the ultimate power will rest with the individual. He must first attain " Swaraj " if he wants to see in reality the full picture of " Village Swaraj ". As is the individual so is the universe. Village Swaraj will thus be the mirror of the spirit of Swaraj which individuals constituting it will manifest in their daily life. Therefore, the Village worker will have to focuss his attention first on the true education. That education should be a harmonious development of three H's—Head, Heart and Hand. Nai Talim is the fruit of Gandhiji's *tapasya*. Gandhiji was an incarnation of the harmonious whole of the three H's. The spirit of non-violence permeates the entire scheme of Nai Talim which aims to make all-round development of the child in body, mind and spirit through handicraft. With the capital equipment of the true education on Nai Talim lines, the citizen will be a great asset in the construction of Village Swaraj.

Village Swaraj is man-centred non-exploiting decentralized, simple village economy providing for full employment to each one of its citizens on the basis of voluntary co-operation and working for achieving self-sufficiency in its basic requirements of food, clothing and other necessities of life.

Modern economic systems rooted as they are in self-indulgence, multiplicity of wants and divorce of ethics from economics are large-scale mechanized, centralized, complicated organizations. They are disfigured by unemployment, under-employment, pauperism, exploitation, a mad race for capturing markets and conquering lands for raw-materials. Competitions, conflicts and class wars corrode the social fabric. They involve enslavement of the individual, treating man only as a hand feeding the machine, reducing him to a mere adjunct of the machine. He loses his fine sensitiveness owing to soul-killing repetitive jobs and consequently rushes to demoralizing cinema theatres, wine shops and prostitution homes for recreation as an escape from the tyranny of the tiring task of the factory. Society is divided into the privileged and the under-privileged, the rich and the poor. Never before was there such economic inequality as is seen today where the multimillionaire is living aimlessly in the lap of luxury and the hard-working toiler has hardly enough to keep his skin and bones together. Highly technically advanced countries like the U. K. and the U. S. A. have yet to solve the problem of unemployment which presents itself to India in a magnified form raised to the nth degree in the context of her vast millions scattered in the seven lakhs of villages mainly living on agriculture from times immemorial.

Village Swaraj is the fruit of life-long search by Gandhiji who having indentified his heart with the starving millions of India has suggested this talisman as an infallible remedy for the ills of India, nay, of the whole world, in whose history the peasantry has always been everywhere exploited and has been on starvation level. In a letter to Pandit Nehru dated 5-10-'45, Gandhiji wrote:

" I am convinced that if India is to attain true freedom and through India the world also, then sooner or later the fact must be recognized that the people will have to live in villages, not in towns, in huts, not in palaces. Crores of people will never be able to live in peace with each other in towns and palaces. They will then have no recourse but to resort to both violence and untruth.

" I hold that without truth and non-violence there can be nothing but destruction for humanity. We can realize truth and non-violence only in the simplicity of village life and this simplicity can best be found in the Charkha and all that the Charkha connotes. I must not fear if the world today is going the wrong way. It may be, that India too will go that way and like the proverbial moth burn itself eventually in the flame round which it dances more and more fiercely. But it is my

bounden duty up to my last breath to try to protect India
and through India the entire world from such a doom.

"The essence of what I have said is that man should
rest content with what are his real needs and become self-
sufficient. If he does not have this control, he cannot save
himself. After all, the world is made up of individuals just
as it is the drops that constitute the ocean . . . . This is a
well-known truth.

Gandhiji thus, stood for simplicity in life and
voluntary poverty. That does not mean that man
should not have creature comforts. He said that every
one should have a balanced diet, necessary clothing and
shelter. He believed that every living being has a right
to food. He observed: "According to me the economic
constitution of India and for the matter of that of the
world, should be such that no one under it should suffer
from want of food and clothing. In other words, everybody should be able to get sufficient work to enable
him to make the two ends meet. And this ideal can be
universally realized only if the means of production of
the elementary necessaries of life remain in the control
of the masses. These should be freely available to all
as God's air and water are or ought to be. They should
not be made a vehicle of traffic for the exploitation of
others. Their monopolization by any country, nation
or group of persons would be unjust. The neglect
of this simple principle is the cause of the destitution
that we witness today not only in this unhappy land
but in other parts of the world too."

To build such a non-violent economy providing
for full employment of all citizens he ruled out industrialism, centralized industries and unnecessary machinery.
He considered cities as agencies exploiting villages.
He even called them boils on the body social of the

country. He suggested that the hope of the future
world order lies in the villages, i. e., small peaceful
co-operatives where there is no compulsion, no force
but where all activities are carried on in voluntary co-
operation. There being the reign of love in the entire
edifice of Village Swaraj, there is none high none low.
All are equal. There will be neither castes nor classes;
no untouchability, no Hindu-Muslim quarrels. All
individuals will be restored to their natural height and
status.

Village Swaraj working in full swing will provide
a model for the world to copy. It will then be a gift
of India to the world. Self-governing village units
of the world will then be a living brotherhood of
highly cultured, intelligent, and vigorous men and
women. To live in this society will itself be an education and a fulfilment. Life therein will be one of self-
expression of all of one's faculties and exchange of
feelings of mutual reverence and love manifested
through acts of mutual service. Culture, art, poetry,
painting and science will find their perfect fulfilment.
It will be the Kingdom of God on earth.

Village Swaraj has such high potentiality in it.
It is for us all to make it dynamic and real. To fulfil
the Dream of the Father of the Nation becomes the
duty of his heirs who have inherited from him a rich
and immortal legacy. It is, therefore, right and proper
that the present State Governments have enacted
legislations to create Gram Panchayats investing them
with larger powers. We hope the Gram Panchayats
will keep before their mind's eye the picture of Village
Swaraj conceived by Gandhiji and work on the lines
laid down by him.

Village Swaraj should be implemented in the spirit in which Gandhiji has conceived it. If the spirit of selfless service and love transcending limits of caste, creed or class is lacking in those who would shoulder the responsibilities of working the Gram Panchayats, Village Swaraj will not yield sweet fruits that Gandhiji expected it to bear.

Let us remember the words of Pandit Nehru in respect of Village systems: "The more a person or a group keeps to himself or itself, the more danger there is of him or it becoming self-centred and selfish and narrow-minded."* Our villages are at present suffering from social discords, casteism and narrowness. The way of making a success of Gram Panchayats is not strewn with roses. The real missionary spirit is expected of village leaders. May the ancient land rise to the occasion and fulfil the mission of India and thereby share the real glory of having worked for the world.

An attempt has been made here to collect together relevant passages from Mahatma Gandhi's writings having a bearing on the subject of Village Swaraj and present his thoughts as far as possible in an uninterrupted manner. To maintain uniformity, indirect narration has been changed to direct speech at a few places. Except for slight editing and omissions, the original text has been faithfully preserved.

I am indebted to Shri Shriman Narayan for writing a Foreword to the compilation.

22-11-'62   H. M. Vyas

---

*Glimpses of World History.

CONTENTS

VILLAGE SWARAJ

TO THE READER

I would like to say to the diligent reader of my writings and to others who are interested in them that I am not at all concerned with appearing to be consistent. In my search after Truth I have discarded many ideas and learnt many new things. Old as I am in age, I have no feeling that I have ceased to grow inwardly or that my growth will stop at the dissolution of the flesh. What I am concerned with is my readiness to obey the call of Truth, my God, from moment to moment, and, therefore, when anybody finds any inconsistency between any two writings of mine, if he has still faith in my sanity, he would do well to choose the later of the two on the same subject.

M. K. GANDHI

Harijan, 29-4-'33, p. 2

CHAPTER 1

THE MEANING OF SWARAJ

The word Swaraj is a sacred word, a Vedic word, meaning self-rule and self-restraint, and not freedom from all restraint which 'independence' often means. *1*

As every country is fit to eat, to drink and to breathe, even so is every nation fit to manage its own affairs, no matter how badly. *2*

By Swaraj I mean the government of India by the consent of the people as ascertained by the largest number of the adult population, male or female, native-born or domiciled, who have contributed by manual labour to the service of the State and who have taken the trouble of having registered their names as voters....Real Swaraj will come not by the acquisition of authority by a few but by the acquisition of the capacity by all to resist authority when it is abused. In other words, Swaraj is to be obtained by educating the masses to a sense of their capacity to regulate and control authority. *3*

By political independence I do not mean an imitation of the British House of Commons or the Soviet rule of Russia or the Fascist rule of Italy or the Nazi rule of Germany. They have systems suited to their genius. We must have ours suited to ours. What that can be is more than I can tell. I have described it as Ramaraj, i.e. sovereignty of the people based on pure moral authority. *4*

Self-government depends entirely upon our internal strength, upon our ability to fight against the heaviest odds. Indeed, self-government which does not require that continuous striving to attain it and to sustain it is not worth the name. I have, therefore, endeavoured to show both in word and deed, that political self-government, that is, self-government for a large number of men and women, is no better than individual self-government, and, therefore, it is to be attained by precisely the same means that are required for individual self-government or self-rule. 5

Self-government means, continuous effort to be independent of government control, whether it is foreign government or whether it is national. Swaraj government will be a sorry affair if people look up to it for the regulation of every detail of life. 6

My Swaraj is to keep intact the genius of our civilization. I want to write many new things but they must all be written on the Indian slate. I would gladly borrow from the West when I can return the amount with decent interest. 7

Swaraj can be maintained, only where there is majority of loyal patriotic people to whom the good of the nation is paramount above all other considerations whatever including their personal profit. Swaraj means government by the many. Where the many are immoral or selfish, their government can spell anarchy and nothing else. 8

The Swaraj of my...our...dream recognizes no race or religious distinctions. Nor is it to be the monopoly of the lettered persons nor yet of moneyed men. Swaraj is to be for all, including the farmer, but emphatically including the maimed, the blind, the starving toiling millions. 9

It has been said that Indian Swaraj will be the rule of the majority community, i.e. the Hindus. There could not be a greater mistake than that. If it were to be true, I for one would refuse to call it Swaraj and would fight it with all the strength at my command, for to me Hind Swaraj is the rule of all people, is the rule of justice. *10*

If Swaraj was not meant to civilize us, and to purify and stabilize our civilization, it would be nothing worth. The very essence of our civilization is that we give a paramount place to morality in all our affairs, public or private. *11*

Poorna Swaraj—'Poorna' complete because it is as much for the prince as for the peasant, as much for the rich landowner as for the landless tiller of the soil, as much for the Hindus as for the Musalmans, as much for Parsis and Christians as for the Jains, Jews and Sikhs, irrespective of any distinction of caste or creed or status in life. *12*

The very connotation of the word and the means of its attainment to which we are pledged—truth and non-violence—precludes all possibility of that Swaraj being more for some one than for the other, being partial to some and prejudicial to others. *13*

The Swaraj of my dream is the poor man's Swaraj. The necessaries of life should be enjoyed by you in common with those enjoyed by the princes and the moneyed men. But that does not mean that they should have palaces like theirs. They are not necessary for happiness. You or I would be lost in them. But you ought to get all the ordinary amenities of life that a rich man enjoys. I have not the slightest doubt that Swaraj is not *Poorna* Swaraj until these amenities are guaranteed to you under it. *14*

My notion of Poorna Swaraj is not isolated independence but healthy and dignified independence. My nationalism, fierce though it is, is not exclusive, is not devised to harm any nation or individual. Legal maxims are not so legal as they are moral. I believe in the eternal truth of *'sic utere tuo ut alienum non laedas'* ('Use thy own property so as not to injure thy neighbour's'). *15*

Complete Independence through truth and non-violence means the independence of every unit, be it the humblest of the nation, without distinction of race, colour or creed. This Independence is never exclusive. It is therefore wholly compatible with inter-dependence within or without. Practice will always fall short of the theory, even as the drawn line falls short of the theoretical line of Euclid. Therefore complete Independence will be complete only to the extent of our approach in practice to truth and non-violence. *16*

It all depends upon what we mean by and want through Poorna Swaraj. If we mean an awakening among the masses, a knowledge among them of their true interest and ability to serve that interest against the whole world and if through Poorna Swaraj we want harmony, freedom from aggression from within or without, and a progressive improvement in the economic condition of the masses, we can gain our end without political power and by directly acting upon the powers that be. *17*

Let there be no mistake about my conception of Swaraj. It is complete independence of alien control and complete economic independence. So at one end you have political independence, at the other the economic. It has two other ends. One of them is moral and social, the corresponding end is Dharma, i.e. religion in the highest sense of the term. It includes Hinduism, Islam, Christianity, etc., but is superior to them all....Let us call this the square of Swaraj, which will be out of shape if any of its angles is untrue. *18*

The Swaraj of my conception will come only when all of us are firmly persuaded that our Swaraj has got to be won, worked and maintained through truth and Ahimsa alone. True democracy or Swaraj of the masses can never come through untruthful and violent means, for the simple reason that the natural corollary to their use would be to remove all opposition through the suppression or extermination of the antagonists. That does not make for individual freedom. Individual freedom can have the fullest play only under a regime of unadulterated Ahimsa. *19*

In Swaraj based on Ahimsa people need not know their rights, but it is necessary for them to know their duties. There is no duty but creates a corresponding right, and those only are true rights which flow from a due performance of one's duties. Hence rights of citizenship accrue only to those who serve the State to which they belong. And they alone can do justice to the rights that accrue to them. Everyone possesses the right to tell lies or resort to *goondaism*. But the exercise of such a right is harmful both to the exerciser and society. But to him who observes truth and non-violence comes prestige, and prestige brings rights. And people who obtain rights as a result of performance of duty, exercise them only for the service of society, never for themselves. Swaraj of a people means the sum total of the Swaraj (self-rule) of individuals. And such Swaraj comes only from performance by individuals of their duty as citizens. In it no one thinks of his rights. They come, when they are needed, for better performance of duty. *20*

Under Swaraj based on non-violence nobody is anybody's enemy, everybody contributes his or her due quota to the common goal, all can read and write, and their knowledge keeps growing from day to day. Sickness and disease are reduced to the minimum. No one is a pauper and labour can always find employment. There is no place under such a government for gambling, drinking and immorality or for class hatred. The rich will use their riches wisely and usefully, and not squander them in increasing their pomp and worldly pleasures. It should not happen that a handful of rich people should live in jewelled palaces and the millions in miserable hovels devoid of sunlight or ventilation. In non-violent Swaraj there can be no encroachment upon just rights; contrariwise no one can possess unjust rights. In a well-organized State, usurpation should be an impossibility and it should be unnecessary to resort to force for dispossessing an usurper. *21*

CHAPTER 2

A PICTURE OF AN IDEAL SOCIETY

[Gandhiji found the picture of his free India in its essentials embodied in a song that was sung at one of his evening prayers in Bhangi Colony, New Delhi. It gripped him. He translated it into English and had it sent to Lord Pethick-Lawrence. It was as follows:]

We are inhabitants of a country
    where there is no sorrow and no suffering,
Where there is no illusion nor anguish,
    no delusion nor desire,
Where flows the Ganges of love
    and the whole creation is full of joy,
Where all minds flow in one direction,
    and where there is no occasion for sense of time,
All have their wants satisfied;
Here all barter is just,
Here all are cast in the same mould,
Here is no lack nor care,
No selfishness in any shape or form,
No high no low, no master no slave;
All is light, yet no burning heat,
That country is within you—
    It is Swaraj, Swadeshi,
The home within you—
    Victory! Victory! Victory!
He realizes it who longs for it. *1*

[What emerged was a picture of the India of his dreams.]

A picture of a casteless and classless society, in which there are no vertical divisions but only horizontal; no high, no low; all service has equal status and carries equal wages; those who have more use their advantage not for themselves but as a trust to serve others who have less; the motivating factor in the choice of vocations is not personal advancement but self-expression and self-realization through the service of society.

Since all service here ranks the same and carries equal wages, hereditary skills are conserved and developed from generation to generation instead of being sacrificed to the lure of personal gain. The principle of community service replaces unrestricted, soulless competition. Everybody is a toiler with ample leisure, opportunity, and facilities for education and culture. It is a fascinating world of cottage crafts and intensive, small-scale farming co-operatives, a world in which there is no room for communalism or caste. Finally, it is the world of Swadeshi in which the economic frontiers are drawn closer but the bounds of individual freedom are enlarged to the maximum limit; everybody is responsible for his immediate environment and all are responsible for society. Rights and duties are regulated by the principle of interdependence, and reciprocity; there is no conflict between the part and the whole; no danger of nationalism becoming narrow, selfish or aggressive or internationalism becoming an abstraction where the concrete is lost in a nebulous haze of vague generalities. 2

There will be neither paupers nor beggars, nor high nor low, neither millionaire employers nor half-starved employees, nor intoxicating drinks or drugs. There will be the same respect for women as vouchsafed to men and the chastity and purity of men and women will be jealously guarded. Where every woman except one's wife, will be treated by men of all religions, as mother, sister or daughter according to her age. Where there will be no untouchability and where there will be equal respect for all faiths. They will be all proudly, joyously and voluntarily bread labourers. I hope everyone who listens to me or reads these lines will forgive me if stretched on my bed and basking in the sun, inhaling life-giving sunshine, I allow myself to indulge in this ecstasy. *3*

CHAPTER 3

WHICH WAY LIES HOPE?

Industrialism

Industrialism is, I am afraid, going to be a curse for mankind. Industrialism depends entirely on your capacity to exploit, on foreign markets being open to you, and on the absence of competitors. It is because these factors are getting less and less every day for England, that its number of unemployed is mounting up daily. The Indian boycott was but a flea-bite. And if that is the state of England, a vast country like India cannot expect to benefit by industrialization. In fact, India, when it begins to exploit other nations —as it must do if it becomes industrialized—will be a curse for other nations, a menace to the world. And why should I think of industrializing India to exploit other nations? Don't you see the tragedy of the situation viz., that we can find work for our 300 millions unemployed, but England can find none for its three millions and is faced with a problem that baffles the greatest intellects of England? The future of industrialism is dark. England has got successful competitors in America, Japan, France, Germany. It has competitors in the handful of mills in India, and as there has been an awakening in India, even so there will be an awakening in South Africa with its vastly richer resources—natural, mineral and human. The mighty English look quite pigmies before the mighty races of Africa. They are noble savages after all, you will say. They are certainly noble, but no savages; and in the course of a few years the Western nations may cease to find in Africa a dumping ground for their wares. And if the future of industrialism is dark for the West, would it not be darker still for India? 1

'What is the cause of the present chaos?' It is exploitation, I will not say, of the weaker nations by the stronger, but of sister nations by sister nations. And my fundamental objection to machinery rests on the fact that it is machinery that has enabled these nations to exploit others. In itself it is wooden thing and can be turned to good purpose or bad. But it is easily turned to a bad purpose as we know. 2

Indeed, the West has had a surfeit of industrialism and exploitation. The fact is that this industrial civilization is a disease because it is all evil. Let us not be deceived by catchwords and phrases. I have no quarrel with steamships and telegraphs. They may stay, if they can, without the support of industrialism and all it connotes. They are not an end. They are in no way indispensable for the permanent welfare of the human race. Now that we know the use of steam and electricity, we should be able to use them on due occasion and after we have learnt to avoid industrialism. Our concern is therefore to destroy industrialism at any cost. 3

There is a growing body of enlightened opinion which distrusts this civilization which has insatiable material ambition at one end and consequent war at the other. But whether good or bad, why must India become industrial in the Western sense? The Western civilization is urban. Small countries like England or Italy may afford to urbanize their systems. A big country like America with a very sparse population, perhaps, cannot do otherwise. But one would think that a big country, with a teeming population with an ancient rural tradition which has hitherto answered its purpose, need not, must not copy the Western model. What is good for one nation situated in one condition is not necessarily good enough for another differently situated. One man's food is often another man's poison. Physical geography of a country has a predominant share in determining its culture. A fur coat may be a necessity for the dweller in the polar regions, it will smother those living in the equatorial regions. 4

The present distress is undoubtedly insufferable. Pauperism must go. But industrialism is no remedy. The evil does not lie in the use of bullock-carts. It lies in our selfishness and want of consideration for our neighbours. If we have no love for our neighbours, no change, however revolutionary, can do us any good. 5

I would destroy that system today, if I had the power. I would use the most deadly weapons, if I believed that they would destroy it. I refrain only because the use of such weapons would only perpetuate the system though it may destroy its present administrators. Those who seek to destroy men rather than manners, adopt the latter and become worse than those whom they destroy under the mistaken belief that the manners will die with the men. They do not know the root of the evil. 6

Industrialism on a mass scale will necessarily lead to passive or active exploitation of the villagers as the problems of competition and marketing come in. Therefore, we have to concentrate on the village being self-contained, manufacturing mainly for use. Provided this character of the industry is maintained, there would be no objection to villagers using even the modern machines and tools that they can make and can afford to use. Only they should not be used as a means of exploitation of others. 7

I do not believe that industrialization is necessary in any case for any country. It is much less so for India. Indeed, I believe that Independent India can only discharge her duty towards a groaning world by adopting a simple but ennobled life by developing her thousands of cottages and living at peace with the world. High thinking is inconsistent with complicated material life based on high speed imposed on us by Mammon worship. All the graces of life are possible only when we learn the art of living nobly.

Whether such plain living is possible for an isolated nation, however large geographically and numerically in the face of a world, armed to the teeth, and in the midst of pomp and circumstance, is a question open to the doubt of a sceptic. The answer is straight and simple. If plain life is worth living, then the attempt is worth making, even though only an individual or a group makes the effort. *8*

European civilization is no doubt suited for the Europeans but it will mean ruin for India, if we endeavour to copy it. This is not to say that we may not adopt and assimilate whatever may be good and capable of assimilation by us as it does not also mean that even the Europeans will not have to part with whatever evil might have crept into it. The incessant search for material comforts and their multiplication is such an evil, and I make bold to say that the Europeans themselves will have to re-model their outlook, if they are not to perish under the weight of the comforts to which they are becoming slaves. It may be that my reading is wrong, but I know that for India to run after the Golden Fleece is to court certain death. Let us engrave on our hearts the motto of a Western philosopher, 'plain living and high thinking'. Today it is certain that the millions cannot have high living and we the few who profess to do the thinking for the masses run the risk, in a vain search after high living, of missing high thinking. *9*

I have heard many of our countrymen say, that we will gain American wealth but avoid its methods. I venture to suggest that such an attempt, if it is made, is foredoomed to failure. We cannot be 'wise, temperate and furious' in a moment. . . . It is not possible to conceive gods inhabiting a land which is made hideous by the smoke and the din of mill chimneys and factories and whose roadways are traversed by rushing engines, dragging numerous cars crowded with men who know not for the most part what they are after, who are often absent-minded, and whose tempers do not improve by being uncomfortably packed like sardines in boxes and finding themselves in the midst of utter strangers, who would oust them if they could and whom they would, in their turn, oust similarly. I refer to these things because they are held to be symbolical of material progress. But they add not an atom to our happiness. *10*

Pandit Nehru wants industrialization, because he thinks that if it is socialized, it would be free from the evils of capitalism. My own view is that the evils are inherent in industrialism, and no amount of socialization can eradicate them. *11*

As I look at Russia where the apotheosis of industrialization has been reached, the life there does not appeal to me. To use the language of the Bible, "What shall it avail a man if he gain the whole world and lose his soul?" In modern terms, it is beneath human dignity to lose one's individuality and become a mere cog in the machine. I want every individual to become a full-blooded, fully developed member of society. The villages must become self-sufficient. I see no other solution if one has to work in terms of Ahimsa. Now I have that conviction. *12*

God forbid that India should ever take to industrialism after the manner of the West. The economic imperialism of a single tiny island kingdom (England) is today keeping the world in chains. If an entire nation of 300 millions took to similar economic exploitation, it would strip the world bare like locusts. *13*

India's destiny lies not along the bloody way of the West, of which she shows signs of tiredness, but along the bloodless way of peace that comes from a simple and godly life. India is in danger of losing her soul. She cannot lose it and live. She must not therefore lazily and helplessly say, 'I cannot escape the onrush from the West.' She must be strong enough to resist it for her own sake and that of the world. *14*

Machinery

'Ideally would you not rule out all machinery?'

Ideally, however, I would rule out all machinery, even as I would reject this very body, which is not helpful to salvation, and seek the absolute liberation of the soul. From that point of view, I would reject all machinery, but machines will remain, because like the body, they are inevitable. The body itself, as I told you, is the purest piece of mechanism; but if it is a hindrance to the highest flights of the soul, it has to be rejected. *15*

Machinery has its place; it has come to stay. But it must not be allowed to displace necessary human labour. An improved plough is a good thing. But if by some chances, one man could plough up by some mechanical invention of his the whole of the land of India, and control all the agricultural produce and if the millions had no other occupation, they would starve, and being idle, they would become dunces, as many have already become. There is hourly danger of many more being reduced to that unenviable state.

I would welcome every improvement in the cottage machine, but I know that it is criminal to displace hand-labour by the introduction of

powerdriven spindles unless one is at the same time
ready to give millions of farmers some other occupation
in their homes. *16*

That use of machinery is lawful which sub-
serves the interest of all. *17*

I would favour the use of the most elaborate
machinery if thereby India's pauperism and resulting idleness be avoided. I have suggested hand-
spinning as the only ready means of driving away
penury and making famine of work and wealth impossible. The spinning wheel itself is a piece of
valuable machinery, and in my own humble way
I have tried to secure improvements in it in keeping
with the special conditions of India. *18*

'Are you against all machinery?'

My answer is emphatically, 'No'. But, I am
against its indiscriminate multiplication. I refuse to
be dazzled by the seeming triumph of machinery.
I am uncompromisingly against all destructive
machinery. But simple tools and instruments and
such machinery as saves individual labour and
lightens the burden of the millions of cottages, I should
welcome. *19*

What I object to, is the *craze* for machinery,
not machinery as such. The *craze* is for what they call
labour-saving machinery. Men go on 'saving
labour', till thousands are without work and thrown
on the open streets to die of starvation. I want to
save time and labour, not for a fraction of mankind, but for all; I want the concentration of
wealth, not in the hands of few, but in the hands of
all. Today machinery merely helps a few to ride on
the back of millions. The impetus behind it all is
not the philanthropy to save labour, but greed. It

is against this constitution of things that I am fighting with all my might.

'Then you are fighting not against machinery as such, but against its abuses which are so much in evidence today.'

I would unhesitatingly say 'yes'; but I would add that scientific truths and discoveries should first of all cease to be mere instruments of greed. Then labourers will not be over-worked and machinery, instead of becoming a hindrance, will be a help. I am aiming, not at eradication of all machinery, but limitation.

'When logically argued out, that would seem to imply that all complicated power-driven machinery should go.'

It might have to go but I must make one thing clear. The supreme consideration is man. The machine should not tend to make atrophied the limbs of man. For instance, I would make intelligent exceptions. Take the case of the Singer Sewing Machine. It is one of the few useful things ever invented, and there is a romance about the device itself. Singer saw his wife labouring over the tedious process of sewing and seaming with her own hands, and simply out of his love for her he devised the Sewing Machine in order to save her from unnecessary labour. He, however, saved not only her labour but also the labour of everyone who could purchase a sewing machine.

'But in that case there would have to be a factory for making these Singer Sewing Machines, and it would have to contain power-driven machinery of ordinary type.'

Yes, but I am socialist enough to say that such factories should be nationalized, or State-controlled. They ought only to be working under the most attractive and ideal conditions, not for profit, but for the benefit of humanity, love taking the place of greed as the motive. It is an alteration in the condition of labour that I want. This mad rush for wealth must cease, and the labourer must be assured, not only of a living wage, but a daily task that is not a mere drudgery. The machine will, under these conditions, be as much a help to the man working it as to the State, or the man who owns it. The present mad rush will cease, and the labourer will work (as I have said) under attractive and ideal conditions. This is but one of the exceptions I have in mind. The Sewing Machine had love at its back. The individual is the one supreme consideration. The saving of labour of the individual should be the object, and honest humanitarian consideration, and not greed, the motive. Replace greed by love and everything will come right. 20

'You are against this machine age, I see.'

To say that is to caricature my views. I am not against machinery as such, but I am totally opposed to it when it masters us.

'You would not industrialize India?'

I would indeed, in my sense of the term. The village communities should be revived. Indian villages produced and supplied to the Indian towns and cities all their wants. India became impoverished when our cities became foreign markets and began to drain the villages dry by dumping cheap and shoddy goods from foreign lands.

'You would then go back to the natural economy?'

Yes. Otherwise I should go back to the city. I am quite capable of running a big enterprise, but I deliberately sacrifice the ambition, not as a sacrifice, but because my heart rebelled against it. For I should have no share in the spoliation of the nation which is going on from day to day. But I am industrializing the village in a different way. *21*

Granting for the moment that machinery may supply all the needs of humanity, still, it would concentrate production in particular areas, so that you would have to go about in a round-about way to regulate distribution, whereas, if there is production and distribution both in the respective areas where things are required, it is automatically regulated, and there is less chance for fraud, none for speculation. . . . When production and consumption both become localized, the temptation to speed up production, indefinitely and at any price, disappears. All the endless difficulties and problems that our present-day economic system presents, too, would then come to an end. . . . Oh yes, mass-production certainly . . . but mass-production (on individual basis) in people's own homes. If you multiply individual production millions of times, would it not give you mass-production on a tremendous scale? . . . Your 'mass-production' is . . . production by the fewest possible number through the aid of highly complicated machinery. . . . My machinery must be of the most elementary type which I can put in the homes of the millions. *22*

I know that man cannot live without industry. Therefore, I cannot be opposed to industrialization.

But I have a great concern about introducing machine industry. The machine produces much too fast, and brings with it a sort of economic system which I cannot grasp. I do not want to accept something when I see its evil effects which outweigh whatever good it brings with it. I want the dumb millions of our land to be healthy and happy and I want them to grow spiritually. As yet for this purpose we do not need the machine. There are many, too many idle hands. But as we grow in understanding, if we feel the need of machines, we certainly will have them. We want industry, let us become industrious. Let us become more self-dependent, then we will not follow the other people's lead so much. We shall introduce machines if and when we need them. Once we shall have shaped our life on Ahimsa, we shall know how to control the machine. *23*

CHAPTER 4

CITIES AND VILLAGES

There are two schools of thought current in the world. One wants to divide the world into cities and the other into villages. The village civilization and the city civilization are totally different things. One depends on machinery and industrialization, and the other on handicrafts. We have given preference to the latter.

After all, this industrialization and large-scale production are only of comparatively recent growth. We don't know how far it has contributed to the development of our happiness, but we know this much that it has brought in its wake the recent world wars. This second world war is not still over, and even if it comes to an end, we are hearing of a third world war. Our country was never so unhappy and miserable as it is at present. City people may be getting big profits and good wages, but all that has become possible by sucking the blood of villages. We don't want to collect lakhs and crores. We don't always want to depend on money for our work. If we are prepared to sacrifice our lives for the cause, money is nothing. We must have faith and we must be true to ourselves. If we have these, we shall be able by decentralizing our capital of Rs. 30 lakhs in villages to create national wealth amounting to Rs. 300 crores. To do that main thing, what is necessary is to make the villages self-sufficient and self-reliant. But mind you, my idea of self-sufficiency is not a narrow one. There is no scope for selfishness and arrogance in my self-sufficiency. 1

We may not be deceived by the wealth to be seen in the cities of India. It does not come from England or America. It comes from the blood of the poorest. There are said to be seven lakhs of villages in India. Some of them have simply been wiped out. No one has any record of those thousands who have died of starvation and disease in Bengal, Karnatak and elsewhere. The Government registers can give no idea of what the village folk are going through. But being a villager myself, I know the condition in the villages. I know village economics. I tell you that the pressure from the top crushes those at the bottom.

All that is necessary is to get off their backs. 2

The workers in the mills of Bombay have become slaves. The condition of the women working in the mills is shocking. When there were no mills, these women were not starving. If the machinery craze grows in our country, it will become an unhappy land. It may be considered a heresy, but I am bound to say that it were better for us to send money to Manchester and to use flimsy Manchester cloth than to multiply mills in India. By using Manchester cloth we only waste our money; but by reproducing Manchester in India, we shall keep our money at the price of our blood, because our very moral being will be sapped, and I call in support of my statement the very mill-hands as witnesses. And those who have amassed wealth out of factories are not likely to be better than other rich men. It would be folly to assume that an Indian Rockfeller would be better than the American Rockfeller. Impoverished India can become free, but it will be hard for any India made rich through immorality to regain its freedom. I fear we shall have to admit that moneyed men support British rule; their interest is bound up with its stability. Money renders a man helpless. The other thing which is equally harmful is sexual vice. Both are poison. A snake-bite is a lesser poison than these two, because the former merely destroys the body but the latter destroy body, mind and soul. We need not, therefore, be pleased with the prospect of the growth of the mill-industry. 3

The poor villagers are exploited by the foreign government and also by their own countrymen— the city-dwellers. They produce the food and go hungry. They produce milk and their children have to go without it. It is disgraceful. Everyone must have a balanced diet, a decent house to live in, facilities for the education of one's children and adequate medical relief. *4*

The half a dozen modern cities are an excrescence and serve at the present moment the evil purpose of draining the life-blood of the villages. . . . The cities with their insolent torts are a constant menace to the life and liberty of the villagers. *5*

It is the city man who is responsible for war all over the world, never the villager. *6*

I regard the growth of cities as an evil thing, unfortunate for mankind and the world, unfortunate for England and certainly unfortunate for India. The British have exploited India through its cities. The latter have exploited the villages. The blood of the villages is the cement with which the edifice of the cities is built. I want the blood that is today inflating the arteries of the cities to run once again in the blood vessels of the villages. *7*

'You have called cities boils or abscesses on the body politic. What should be done with these boils?'

If you ask a doctor he will tell you what to do with a boil. It has to be cured either by lancing or by the application of plasters and poultices. Edward Carpenter called civilization a malady which needed a cure. The growth of big cities is only a symptom of that malady. Being a nature curist, I am naturally in favour of nature's way of cure by a general purification of the system. If the hearts of the city-dwellers remain rooted in the villages, if they become truly village-minded, all other things will automatically follow and the boil will quickly heal. *8*

I have believed and repeated times without number that India is to be found not in its few cities but in its 7,00,000 villages. But we town-dwellers have believed that India is to be found in its towns and the villages were created to minister to our needs. We have hardly ever paused to inquire if those poor folk get sufficient to eat and clothe themselves with and whether they have a roof to shelter themselves from sun and rain. *9*

I have found that the town-dweller has generally exploited the villager, in fact he has lived on the poor villager's subsistence. Many a British official has written about the conditions of the people of India. No one has, to my knowledge, said that the Indian villager has enough to keep body and soul together. On the contrary they have admitted that the bulk of the population live on the verge of starvation and ten per cent are semi-starved, and that millions have to rest content with a pinch of dirty salt and chillies and polished rice or parched grain.

You may be sure that if any of us were to be asked to live on that diet, we should not expect to survive it longer than a month or should be afraid of losing our mental faculties. And yet our villagers go through that state from day to day. *10*

Over 75 per cent of the population are agriculturists. But there cannot be much spirit of self-government about us if we take away or allow others to take away from them almost the whole of the result of their labour. *11*

The cities are capable of taking care of themselves. It is the village we have to turn to. We have to disabuse them of their prejudice, their superstitions, their narrow outlook and we can do so in no other manner than that of staying amongst them and sharing their joys and sorrows and spreading education and intelligent information among them. *12*

We have got to be ideal villagers, not the villagers with their queer ideas about sanitation and giving no thought to how they eat and what they eat. Let us not, like most of them, cook anyhow, eat anyhow, live anyhow. Let us show them the ideal diet. Let us not go by mere likes and dislikes, but get at the root of those likes and dislikes. *13*

We must identify ourselves with the villagers who toil under the hot sun beating on their bent backs and see how we would like to drink water from the pool in which the villagers bathe, wash their clothes and pots, in which their cattle drink and roll. Then and not till then shall we truly represent the masses and they will, as surely as I am writing this, respond to every call. *14*

We have got to show them that they can grow their vegetables, their greens, without much expense, and keep good health. We have also to show that most of the vitamins are lost when they cook the leaves. *15*

We have to teach them how to economize time, health and money. Lionel Curtis described our villages as dung-heaps. We have to turn them into model villages. Our village-folk do not get fresh air though they are surrounded by fresh air; they don't get fresh food though they are surrounded by the freshest foods. I am talking like a missionary in this matter of food, because my mission is to make villages a thing of beauty. *16*

It is profitless to find out whether the villages of India were always what they are today. If they were

never better it is a reflection upon the ancient culture
in which we take so much pride. But if they were
never better, how is it that they have survived
centuries of decay which we see going on around us.
. . . The task before every lover of the country is
how to prevent this decay or, which is the same thing,
how to reconstruct the villages of India so that it
may be as easy for anyone to live in them as it is
supposed to be in the cities. Indeed, it is the task
before every patriot. It may be that the villagers
are beyond redemption, that rural civilization has
had its day and that the seven hundred thousand
villages have to give place to seven hundred well-
ordered cities supporting a population not of three
hundred millions but thirty. If such is to be, India's
fate, even that won't come in a day. It must take
time to wipe out a number of villages and villagers
and transform the remainder into cities and
citizens. *17*

The village movement is as much an education
of the city people as of the villagers. Workers drawn
from cities have to develop village mentality and
learn the art of living after the manner of villagers.
This does not mean that they have to starve like the
villagers. But it does mean that there must be a
radical change in the old style of life. *18*

The only way is to sit down in their midst and
work away in steadfast faith, as their scavengers,
their nurses, their servants, not as their patrons, and
to forget all our prejudices and prepossessions. Let
us for a moment forget even Swaraj, and certainly
forget the 'haves' whose presence oppresses us at
every step. They are there. There are many who are
dealing with these big problems. Let us tackle the

humbler work of the village which is necessary now and would be even after we have reached our goal. Indeed, the village work when it becomes successful will itself bring us nearer the goal. *19*

The village communities should be revived. Indian villages produced and supplied to the Indian towns and cities all their wants. India became impoverished when our cities became foreign markets and began to drain the villages dry by dumping cheap and shoddy goods from foreign lands. *20*

It is only when the cities realize the duty of making an adequate return to the villages for the strength and sustenance which they derive from them, instead of selfishly exploiting them, that a healthy and moral relationship between the two will spring up. And if the city children are to play their part in this great and noble work of social reconstruction, the vocations through which they are to receive their education ought to be directly related to the requirements of the villages. *21*

We are inheritors of a rural civilization. The vastness of our country, the vastness of the population, the situation and the climate of the country have in my opinion, destined it for a rural civilization. Its defects are well known, but not one of them is irremediable. To uproot it and substitute for it an urban civilization seems to me an impossibility, unless we are prepared by some drastic means to reduce the population from three hundred million to three or say even thirty. I can therefore suggest remedies on the assumption that we must perpetuate the present rural civilization and endeavour to rid it of its acknowledged defects. *22*

CHAPTER 5

VILLAGE SWARAJ

The Place of Villages

To serve our villages is to establish Swaraj. Everything else is but an idle dream. *1*

If the village perishes India will perish too. It will be no more India. Her own mission in the world will get lost. *2*

We have to make a choice between India of the villages that are as ancient as herself and India of the cities which are a creation of foreign domination. Today the cities dominate and drain the villages so that they are crumbling to ruin. My Khadi mentality tells me that cities must subserve villages when that domination goes. Exploiting of villages is itself organized violence. If we want Swaraj to be built on non-violence, we will have to give the villages their proper place. *3*

I am convinced that if India is to attain true freedom and through India the world also, then sooner or later the fact must be recognized that people will have to live in villages, not in towns, in huts, not in palaces. Crores of people will never be able to live at peace with each other in towns and palaces. They will then have no recourse but to resort to both violence and untruth.

I hold that without truth and non-violence there can be nothing but destruction for humanity. We can realize truth and non-violence only in the simplicity of village life and this simplicity can best be found in the *charkha* and all that the *charkha*

30

connotes. I must not fear if the world today is going
the wrong way. It may be that India too will go
that way and like the proverbial moth burn itself
eventually in the flame round which it dances more
and more fiercely. But it is my bounden duty up to
my last breath to try to protect India and through
India the entire world from such a doom. *4*

Village Swaraj

My idea of Village Swaraj is that it is a complete
republic, independent of its neighbours for its own
vital wants, and yet interdependent for many others
in which dependence is a necessity. Thus every
village's first concern will be to grow its own food
crops and cotton for its cloth. It should have a reserve
for its cattle, recreation and playground for adults and
children. Then if there is more land available, it will
grow *useful* money crops, thus excluding *ganja*,
tobacco, opium and the like. The village will maintain
a village theatre, school and public hall. It will have
its own waterworks ensuring clean water supply. This
can be done through controlled wells or tanks. Education will be compulsory up to the final basic course.
As far as possible every activity will be conducted on
the co-operative basis. There will be no castes such
as we have today with their graded untouchability.
Non-violence with its technique of Satyagraha and
non-co-operation will be the sanction of the village
community. There will be a compulsory service of
village guards who will be selected by rotation from
the register maintained by the village. The government of the village will be conducted by the Panchayat
of five persons annually elected by the adult villagers,
male and female, possessing minimum prescribed

qualifications. These will have all the authority and
jurisdiction required. Since there will be no system
of punishments in the accepted sense, this Panchayat
will be the legislature, judiciary and executive combined to operate for its year of office. Any village can
become such a republic today without much interference, even from the present Government whose sole
effective connection with the villages is the exaction
of the village revenue. I have not examined here the
question of relations with the neighbouring villages
and the centre if any. My purpose is to present an
outline of village government. Here there is perfect
democracy based upon individual freedom. The individual is the architect of his own government. The
law of non-violence rules him and his government. He
and his village are able to defy the might of a world.
For the law governing every villager is that he will
suffer death in the defence of his and his village's
honour.

There is nothing inherently impossible in the
picture drawn here. To model such a village may be
the work of a life time. Any lover of true democracy
and village life can take up a village, treat it as his
world and sole work, and he will find good result. He
begins by being the village scavenger, spinner, watch-
man, medicine man and school-master all at once. If
nobody comes near him, he will be satisfied with
scavenging and spinning. 5

An Ideal Village

An ideal Indian village will be so constructed as
to lend itself to perfect sanitation. It will have cottages
with sufficient light and ventilation built of a material
obtainable within a radius of five miles of it. The

cottages will have courtyards enabling householders to plant vegetables for domestic use and to house their cattle. The village lanes and streets will be free of all avoidable dust. It will have wells according to its needs and accessible to all. It will have houses of worship for all, also a common meeting place, a village common for grazing its cattle, a co-operative dairy, primary and secondary schools in which industrial education will be the central fact, and it will have Panchayats for settling disputes. It will produce its own grains, vegetables and fruit, and its own Khadi. This is roughly my idea of a model village....I am convinced that the villagers can, under intelligent guidance, double the village income as distinguished from individual income. There are in our villages inexhaustible resources not for commercial purposes in every case but certainly for local purposes in almost every case. The greatest tragedy is the hopeless unwillingness of the villagers to better their lot.

The very first problem the village worker will solve is its sanitation. It is the most neglected of all the problems that baffle workers and that undermine physical wellbeing and breed disease. If the worker became a voluntary *bhangi*, he would begin by collecting night-soil and turning it into manure and sweeping village streets. He will tell people how and where they should perform daily functions and speak to them on the value of sanitation and the great injury caused by its neglect. The worker will continue to do the work whether the villagers listen to him or no. 6

My ideal village will contain intelligent human beings. They will not live in dirt and darkness as animals. Men and women will be free and able to hold their own against anyone in the world. There will be neither plague, nor cholera, nor smallpox; no one will be idle, no one will wallow in luxury. Everyone will have to contribute his quota of manual labour....It is possible to envisage railways, post and telegraph...and the like....7

CHAPTER 6

BASIC PRINCIPLES OF VILLAGE SWARAJ

1. Supremacy of Man—Full Employment

The supreme consideration is man. 1

The end to be sought is human happiness combined with full mental and moral growth. I use the adjective moral as synonymous with spiritual. This end can be achieved under decentralization. Centralization as a system is inconsistent with a non-violent structure of society. 2

According to me the economic constitution of India and for the matter of that of the world, should be such that no one under it should suffer from want of food and clothing. In other words everybody should be able to get sufficient work to enable him to make the two ends meet. And this ideal can be universally realized only if the means of production of the elementary necessaries of life remain in the control of the masses. These should be freely available to all as God's air and water are or ought to be; they should not be made a vehicle of traffic for the exploitation of others. Their monopolization by any country, nation or group of persons would be unjust. The neglect of this simple principle is the cause of the destitution that we witness today not only in this unhappy land but in other parts of the world too. *3*

That economics is untrue which ignores or disregards moral values. The extension of the law of non-violence in the domain of economics means nothing less than the introduction of moral values as a factor to be considered in regulating international commerce. *4*

Every human being has a right to live, and therefore to find the wherewithal to feed himself and where necessary, to clothe and house himself. *5*

'Take no thought for the morrow' is an injunction which finds an echo in almost all the religious scriptures of the world. In well-ordered society the securing of one's livelihood should be and is found to be the easiest thing in the world. Indeed, the test of orderliness in a country is not the number of millionaires it owns, but the absence of starvation among its masses. *6*

Any plan which exploited the raw materials of a country and neglected the pontentially more powerful man-power was lop-sided and could never tend to establish human equality.

Real planning consisted in the best utilization of the whole man-power of India. *7*

We should be ashamed of resting or having a square meal so long as there is one able-bodied man or woman without work or food. *8*

Every man has an equal right to the necessaries of life even as birds and beasts have. And since every right carries with it a corresponding duty and the corresponding remedy for resisting any attack upon it, it is merely a matter of finding out the corresponding duties and remedies to vindicate the elementary fundamental equality. The corresponding duty is to labour with my limbs and the corresponding remedy is to non-co-operate with him who deprives me of the fruit of my labour. *9*

2. Body-labour

How can a man who does not do body labour, have the right to eat? *10*

'Earn thy bread by the sweat of thy brow,' says the Bible. Sacrifices may be of many kinds. One of them may well be Bread labour. If all laboured for their bread and no more, then there would be enough food and enough leisure for all. Then there would be no cry of over-population, no disease and no such misery as we see around. Such labour will be the highest form of sacrifice. Men will no doubt do many other things either through their bodies or through their minds, but all this will be labour of love for the common good. There will then be no rich and no poor, none high and none low, no touchable and no untouchable. *11*

The hungry millions ask for one poem—invigorating food. They cannot be given it. They must earn it. And they can earn only by the sweat of their brow. *12*

Return to the villages means a definite voluntary recognition of the duty of Bread labour and all it connotes. *13*

Intellectual work is important and has an undoubted place in the scheme of life. But what I insist on is the necessity of physical labour. No man, I claim, ought to be free from that obligation. *14*

God created man to work for his food and said that those who ate without work were thieves. *15*

3. Equality

True economics never militates against the highest ethical standard, just as all true ethics to be worth its name must at the same time be also good economics. An economics that inculcates Mammon worship, and enables the strong to amass wealth at the expense of the weak, is a false and dismal science. It spells death. True economics, on the other hand, stands for social justice, it promotes the good of all equally including the weakest, and is indispensable for decent life. *16*

I want to bring about an equalization of status. *17*

My ideal is equal distribution, but so far as I can see, it is not to be realized. I therefore work for equitable distribution. *18*

Economic equality is the master key to non-violent independence. Working for economic equality means abolishing the eternal conflict between capital and labour. It means the levelling down of the few rich in whose hands is concentrated the bulk of the nation's wealth on the one hand, and a levelling up of the semi-starved naked millions on the other. A non-violent system of government is clearly an impossibility so long as the wide gulf between the rich and the hungry millions persists. The contrast between the palaces of New Delhi and the miserable hovels of the poor, labouring class cannot last one day in a free India in which the poor will enjoy the same power as the richest in the land. A violent and bloody revolution is a certainty one day unless there is a voluntary abdication of riches and the power that riches give and sharing them for the common good. I adhere to my doctrine of trusteeship in spite of the ridicule that has been poured upon it. It is true that it is difficult to reach. So is non-violence difficult to attain. But we made up our minds in 1920 to negotiate that steep ascent. *19*

The real implication of equal distribution is that each man shall have the wherewithal to supply all his natural wants and no more. For example, if one man has a weak digestion and requires only a quarter of a pound of flour for his bread and another needs a pound, both should be in a position to satisfy their wants. To bring this ideal into being the entire social order has got to be reconstructed. A society based on non-violence cannot nurture any other ideal. We may not perhaps be able to realize the goal, but we must bear it in mind and work unceasingly to near it. To the same extent as we progress towards our goal we shall find contentment and happiness, and to that extent too, shall we have contributed towards the bringing into being of a non-violent society.

4. Trusteeship

Indeed at the root of this doctrine of equal distribution must lie that of the trusteeship of the wealthy for superfluous wealth possessed by them. For according to the doctrine they may not possess a rupee more than their neighbours. How is this to be brought about? Non-violently? Or should the wealthy be dispossessed of their possessions? To do this we would naturally have to resort to violence. This violent action cannot benefit society. Society will be the poorer, for it will lose the gifts of a man who knows how to accumulate wealth. Therefore non-violent way is evidently superior. The rich man will be left in possession of his wealth, of which he will use what he reasonably requires for his personal needs and will act as a trustee for the remainder to be used for the society. In this argument, honesty on the part of the trustee is assumed.

If however, in spite of the utmost effort, the rich do not become guardians of the poor in the true sense of the term and the latter are more and more crushed and die of hunger, what is to be done? In trying to find out the solution of this riddle I have lighted on non-violent non-co-operation and civil disobedience as the right and infallible means. The rich cannot accumulate wealth without the co-operation of the poor in society. If this knowledge were to penetrate to and spread amongst the poor, they would become strong and would learn how to free themselves by means of non-violence from the crushing inequalities which have brought them to the verge of starvation. 20

5. Decentralization

I suggest that, if India is to evolve along non-violent lines, it will have to decentralize many things. Centralization cannot be sustained and defended without adequate force. Simple homes from which there is nothing to take away require no policing; the palaces of the rich must have strong guards to protect them against dacoity. So must huge factories. Rurally organized India will run less risk of foreign invasion than urbanized India, well equipped with military, naval and air forces. 21

You cannot build non-violence on a factory civilization, but it can be built on self-contained villages. Rural economy as I have conceived it, eschews exploitation altogether, and exploitation is the essence of violence. 22

6. Swadeshi

Swadeshi is that spirit in us which restricts us to the use and service of our immediate surroundings to the exclusion of the more remote.

If we follow the Swadeshi doctrine, it would be your duty and mine to find out neighbours who can supply our wants and to teach them to supply them where they do not know how to proceed, assuming that there are neighbours who are in want of healthy occupation. Then every village of India will almost be a self-supporting and self-contained unit, exchanging only such necessary commodities with other villages as are not locally producible. This may all sound nonsensical. Well, India is a country of nonsense. It is nonsensical to parch one's throat with thirst when a kindly Mohammedan is ready to offer pure water to drink. And yet thousands of Hindus would rather die of thirst than drink water from a Mohammedan household. These nonsensical men can also, once they are convinced that their religion demands that they should wear garments manufactured in India only and eat food only grown in India, decline to wear any other clothing or eat any other food. 23

A true votary of Swadeshi will not harbour ill-will towards a foreigner and not be actuated by antagonism towards anybody on the earth. Swadeshi is not a cult of hatred. It is a doctrine of selfless service that has its roots in the purest Ahimsa, i.e., love. 24

7. Self-sufficiency

The unit of society should be a village or call it a manageable small group of people who would, in the ideal, be self-sufficient (in the matter of their vital requirements) as a unit. 25

Every village's first concern will be to grow its own food crops, and cotton for its cloth. 26

The central fact of Khaddar is to make every village self-supporting for its food and clothing.

Self-sufficient Khadi will never succeed without cotton being grown by spinners themselves or practically in every village. It means decentralization of cotton cultivation so far at least as self-sufficient Khadi is concerned. 27

Every village has to be self-sustained and capable of managing its affairs even to the extent of defending itself against the whole world. 28

8. Co-operation

As far as possible every activity will be conducted on the co-operative basis. 29

The system of co-operation was far more necessary for the agriculturists than for the mat-weavers. The land belonged to the State; therefore, it yielded the largest return when it was worked co-operatively.

Let it be remembered that co-operation should be based on strict non-violence. 30

9. Satyagraha

Non-violence with its technique of Satyagraha and non-co-operation will be the sanction of the village community. 31

10. Equality of Religions

Every religion has its full and equal place. We are all leaves of a majestic tree whose trunk cannot be shaken off its roots which are deep down in the bowels of the earth. The mightiest of winds cannot move it. 32

11. Panchayat Raj

The government of the village will be conducted by the Panchayat of five persons, annually elected by the adult villagers, male and female, possessing minimum prescribed qualifications. *33*

Since there will be no system of punishments in the accepted sense, this Panchayat will be the legislature, judiciary and executive combined to operate for its year of office. *34*

Every Panchayat of five adult men or women being villagers or village-minded shall form a unit.

Two such contiguous Panchayats shall form a working party under a leader elected from among themselves.

When there are one hundred such Panchayats, the fifty first grade leaders shall elect from among themselves a second grade leader and so on, the first grade leaders meanwhile working under the second grade leader. Parallel groups of two hundred Panchayats shall continue to be formed till they cover the whole of India, each succeeding group of Panchayats electing second grade leader after the manner of the first. All second grade leaders shall serve jointly for the whole of India and severally for their respective areas. The second grade leaders may elect, whenever they deem necessary, from among themselves a chief who will, during pleasure, regulate and command all the groups. *35*

12. Nai Talim

By education I mean an all-round drawing out of the best in child and man—body, mind and spirit. Literacy is not the end of education nor even the beginning. It is only one of the means whereby man and woman can be educated. Literacy in itself is no education. I would therefore begin the child's education by teaching it a useful handicraft and enabling it to produce from the moment it begins its training. Thus every school can be made self-supporting, the condition being that the State takes over the manufactures of these schools. *36*

CHAPTER 7

BREAD LABOUR

The great Nature has intended us to earn our bread in the sweat of our brow. Everyone, therefore, who idles away a single minute becomes to that extent a burden upon his neighbours, and to do so is to commit a breach of the very first lesson of Ahimsa....Ahimsa is nothing if not a well-balanced exquisite consideration for one's neighbour, and an idle man is wanting in that elementary consideration. *1*

The divine law, that man must earn his bread by labouring with his own hands, was first stressed by a Russian writer named T. M. Bondaref. Tolstoy advertised it and gave it wide publicity. In my view the same principle has been set forth in the third chapter of the Gita, where we are told, that he who eats without offering sacrifice eats stolen food. Sacrifice here can only mean bread labour.

Reason too leads to an identical conclusion. How can a man, who does not do body labour, have the right to eat? 'In the sweat of thy brow shalt thou eat thy bread', says the Bible. A millionaire cannot carry on for long, and will soon get tired of his life, if he rolls in his bed all day long, and is even helped to his food. He, therefore, induces hunger by exercise and helps himself to the food he eats. If everyone, whether rich or poor, has thus to take exercise in some shape or form, why should it not assume the form of productive, i.e. bread labour ? No one asks the cultivator to take breathing exercise or to work his muscles. And more than nine-tenths of humanity lives by tilling the soil. How much happier, healthier and more peaceful would the world become, if the remaining tenth followed the example of the overwhelming majority, at least to the extent of labouring enough for their food!

There is a world-wide conflict between capital and labour, and the poor envy the rich. If all worked for their bread, distinctions of rank would be obliterated; the rich would still be there, but they would deem themselves only trustees of their property, and would use it mainly in the public interest.

Bread labour is a veritable blessing to one who would observe non-violence, worship Truth and make the observance of Brahmacharya a natural act. This labour can truly be related to agriculture alone. But at present at any rate, everybody is not in a position to take to it. A person can therefore spin or weave, or take up carpentry or smithery, instead of tilling the soil, always regarding agriculture, however, to be the ideal. Every one must be his own scavenger. Evacuation is as necessary as eating: and the best thing would be for every one to dispose of his own waste. If this is impossible, each family should see to its own scavenging.

I have felt for years, that there must be something radically wrong, where scavenging has been made the concern of a separate class in society. We have no historical record of the man who first assigned the lowest status to this essential sanitary service. Whoever he was, he by no means did us a good. We should, from our very childhood, have the idea impressed upon our minds that we are all scavengers, and the easiest way of doing so is, for every one who has realized this, to commence bread-labour as a scavenger. Scavenging, thus intelligently taken up, will help to a true appreciation of the equality of man. 2

The true source of rights is duty. If we all discharge our duties, rights will not be far to seek. If leaving duties unperformed we run after rights, they escape us like a will-o'-the-wisp. The more we pursue them, the farther they fly. The same teaching has been embodied by Krishna in the immortal words: 'Action alone is thine. Leave thou the fruit severely alone.' Action is duty: fruit is the right. 3

Every man has an equal right to the necessaries of life even as birds and beasts have. And since every right carries with it a corresponding duty and the corresponding remedy for resisting any attack upon it, it is merely a matter of finding out the corresponding duties and remedies to vindicate the elementary fundamental equality. The corresponding duty is to labour with my limbs and the corresponding remedy is to non-co-operate with him who deprives me of the fruit of my labour. 4

If all laboured for their bread and no more, then there would be enough food and enough leisure for all. Then there would be no cry of over-population; no disease and no such misery as we see around. Such labour will be the highest form of sacrifice. Men will no doubt do many other things either through their bodies or through their minds, but all this will be labour of love for the common good. There will then be no rich and no poor, none high and none low, no touchable and no untouchable.

This may be an unattainable ideal. But we need not, therefore, cease to strive for it. Even if, without fulfilling the whole law of sacrifice, that is, the law of our being, we performed physical labour enough for our daily bread, we should go a long way towards the ideal.

If we did so, our wants would be minimized, our food would be simple. We should then eat to live, not live to eat. Let anyone who doubts the accuracy of this proposition try to sweat for his bread, he will derive the greatest relish from the productions of his labour, improve his health, and discover that many things he took were superfluities. 5

Intelligent bread labour is any day the highest form of social service.

The adjective 'intelligent' has been prefixed to labour in order to show that labour to be social service must have that definite purpose behind it. Otherwise every labourer can be said to render social service. He does in a way, but what is meant here is something much more than that. A person who labours for the general good of all serves society and is worthy of his hire. Therefore, such bread labour is not different from social service. 6

May not men earn their bread by intellectual labour? No. The needs of the body must be supplied by the body. "Render unto Caesar that which is Caesar's" perhaps applies here well. Mere mental, that is, intellectual labour is for the soul and is its own satisfaction. It should never demand payment. In the ideal state, doctors, lawyers and the like will work solely for the benefit of society, not for self. Obedience to the law of bread labour will bring about a silent revolution in the structure of society. Man's triumph will consist in substituting the struggle for existence by the struggle for mutual service. The law of the brute will be replaced by the law of man.

Return to the villages means a definite, voluntary recognition of the duty of bread labour and all it connotes. But says the critic, "Millions of India's children are today living in the villages and yet they are living a life of semi-starvation." This, alas, is but too true. Fortunately we know that theirs is not voluntary obedience. They would perhaps shirk body labour if they could, and even rush to the nearest city if they could be accommodated in it. Compulsory obedience to a master is a state of slavery, willing obedience to one's father is the glory of sonship. Similarly compulsory obedience to the law of bread labour breeds poverty, disease and discontent. It is a state of slavery. Willing obedience to it must bring contentment and health. And it is health which is real wealth, not pieces of silver and gold. 7

Beggary

My Ahimsa would not tolerate the idea of giving a free meal to a healthy person who has not worked for it in some honest way, and if I had the power, I would stop every *sadavrata* where free meals are given. It has degraded the nation and it has encouraged laziness, idleness, hypocrisy and even crime. Such misplaced charity adds nothing to the wealth of the country, whether material or spiritual, and gives a false sense of meritoriousness to the donor. How nice

and wise it would be if the donor were to open institutions where they would give meals under healthy,
clean surroundings to men and women who would
work for them. I personally think that the spinning
wheel or any of the processes that cotton has to go
through will be an ideal occupation. But if they will
not have that, they may choose any other work; only
the rule should be "No labour, no meal". Every city
has its own difficult problem of beggars, a problem
for which the moneyed men are responsible. I know
that it is easier to fling free meals in the faces of idlers,
but much more difficult to organize an institution
where honest work has to be done before meals are
served. From a pecuniary standpoint, in the initial
stages at any rate, the cost of feeding people after
taking work from them will be more than the cost of
the present free kitchens. But I am convinced that it
will be cheaper in the long run, if we do not want to
increase in geometrical progression the race of loafers
which is fast over-running this land. *8*

I do feel that whilst it is bad to encourage begging,
I will not send away a beggar without offering him
work and food. If he does not work, I shall let him
go without food. Those who are physically disabled
like the halt and the maimed have got to be supported
by the State. There is, however, a lot of fraud going
on under cover of pretended blindness or even genuine
blindness. So many blind have become rich because of
ill-gotten gains. It would be a good thing if they were
taken to an asylum, rather than be exposed to this
temptation. *9*

CHAPTER 8

EQUALITY

My idea of society is that while we are born equal meaning that we have a right to equal opportunity, all have not the same capacity. It is, in the nature of things, impossible. For instance, all cannot have the same height, or colour or degree of intelligence, etc.; therefore in the nature of things, some will have ability to earn more and others less. People with talents will have more, and they will utilize their talents for this purpose. If they utilize their talents kindly, they will be performing the work of the State. Such people exist as trustees, on no other terms. I would allow a man of intellect to earn more, I would not cramp his talent. But the bulk of his greater earnings must be used for the good of the State, just as the incomes of all earning sons of the father go to the common family fund. *1*

The real implication of equal distribution is that each man shall have the wherewithal to supply all his natural wants and no more. For example, if one man has a weak digestion and requires only a quarter of a pound of flour for his bread and another needs a pound, both should be in a position to satisfy their wants. To bring this ideal into being the entire social order has got to be reconstructed. A society based on non-violence cannot nurture any other ideal. We may not perhaps be able to realize the goal, but we must bear it in mind and work unceasingly to near it. To the same extent as we progress towards our goal we shall find contentment and happiness, and to that

49

extent too, shall we have contributed towards the bringing into being of a non-violent society. 2

Equality of Income

Put your talents in the service of the country instead of converting them into £. s. d. If you are a medical man, there is disease enough in India to need all your medical skill. If you are a lawyer, there are differences and quarrels enough in India. Instead of fomenting more trouble, patch up those quarrels and stop litigation. If you are an engineer, build model houses suited to the means and needs of our people and yet full of health and fresh air. There is nothing that you have learnt which cannot be turned to account. (The friend who asked the question was a Chartered Accountant and Gandhiji then said to him:) There is a dire need everywhere for accountants to audit the accounts of Congress and its adjunct associations. Come to India—I will give you enough work and also your hire—4 annas per day which is surely much more than millions in India get. 3

Practice of law ought not to mean taking more daily than, say, a village carpenter's wage. 4

If India was to live an exemplary life of independence which would be the envy of the world, all the *bhangis*, doctors, lawyers, teachers, merchants and others would get the same wages for an honest day's work. Indian society may never reach the goal but it was the duty of every Indian to set his sail towards that goal and no other if India was to be a happy land. 5

CHAPTER 9

THEORY OF TRUSTEESHIP

Supposing I have come by a fair amount of wealth either by way of legacy, or by means of trade and industry, I must know that all that wealth does not belong to me, what belongs to me is the right to an honourable livelihood, no better than that enjoyed by millions of others. The rest of my wealth belongs to the community and must be used for the welfare of the community. I enunciated this theory when the Socialist theory was placed before the country in respect to the possessions held by zamindars and ruling chiefs. They would do away with these privileged classes. I want them to outgrow their greed and sense of possession, and to come down in spite of their wealth to the level of those who earn their bread by labour. The labourer has to realize that the wealthy man is less owner of his wealth than the labourer is owner of *his* own, viz. the power to work.

The question how many can be real trustees according to this definition is beside the point. If the theory is true, it is immaterial whether many live up to it or only one man lives up to it. The question is of conviction. If you accept the principle of Ahimsa, you have to strive to live up to it, no matter whether you succeed or fail. There is nothing in this theory which can be said to be beyond the grasp of intellect, though you may say it is difficult of practice *1*

You may say that trusteeship is a legal fiction. But if people meditate over it constantly and try to

act up to it, then life on earth would be governed
far more by love than it is at present. Absolute
trusteeship is an abstraction like Euclid's definition
of a point, and is equally unattainable. But if we
strive for it, we shall be able to go further in realizing a state of equality on earth than by any other
method. . . . It is my firm conviction that if the
State suppressed capitalism by violence, it will be
caught in the coils of violence itself, and fail to develop non-violence at any time. The State represents
violence in a concentrated and organized form. The
individual has a soul, but as the State is a soulless
machine, it can never be weaned from violence to
which it owes its very existence. Hence I prefer the
doctrine of trusteeship. The fear is always there that
the State may use too much violence against those
who differ from it. I would be very happy indeed
if the people concerned behaved as trustees; but if
they fail, I believe we shall have to deprive them of
their possessions through the State with the minimum exercise of violence. . . . (That is why I said
at the Round Table Conference that every vested
interest must be subjected to scrutiny, and confis-
cation ordered where necessary. . . with or without compensation as the case demanded.) What I
would personally prefer would be not a centralization of power in the hands of the State, but an extension of the sense of trusteeship; as in my opinion the
violence of private ownership is less injurious than
the violence of the State. However, if it is unavoidable, I would support a minimum of State-
ownership. 2

It has become the fashion these days to say that
society cannot be organized or run on non-violent

lines. I join issue on that point. In a family, when the father slaps his delinquent child, the latter does not think of retaliating. He obeys his father not because of the deterrent effect of the slap but because of the offended love which he senses behind it. That in my opinion is an epitome of the way in which society is or should be governed. What is true of the family must be true of society which is but a larger family. 3

I hold that non-violence is not merely a personal virtue. It is also a social virtue to be cultivated like the other virtues. Surely society is largely regulated by the expression of non-violence in its mutual dealings. What I ask for is an extension of it on a larger, national and international scale. 4

My theory of 'trusteeship' is no make-shift, certainly no camouflage. I am confident that it will survive all other theories. It has the sanction of philosophy and religion behind it. That possessors of wealth have not acted up to the theory does not prove its falsity; it proves the weakness of the wealthy. No other theory is compatible with non-violence. In the non-violent method the wrong-doer compasses his own end, if he does not undo the wrong. For, either through non-violent non-co-operation he is made to see the error, or he finds himself completely isolated. 5

I have no hesitation in endorsing the opinion that generally rich men and for that matter most men are not particular as to the way they make money. In the application of the method of non-violence, one must believe in the possibility of every person, however, depraved, being reformed under humane and skilled treatment. We must appeal to the good

in human beings and expect response. Is it not conducive to the wellbeing of society that every member
uses all his talents, only not for personal aggrandize-
ment but for the good of all? We do not want to
produce a dead equality where every person becomes
or is rendered incapable of using his ability to the utmost possible extent. Such a society must ultimately
perish. I therefore suggest that my advice that
moneyed men may earn their crores (honestly only,
of course) but so as to dedicate them to the service of
all is perfectly sound. "तेन त्यक्तेन भुंजीथा:" is a *mantra*
based on uncommon knowledge. It is the surest
method to evolve a new order of life of universal
benefit in the place of the present one where each one
lives for himself without regard to what happens to
his neighbour. *6*

CHAPTER 10

SWADESHI

Swadeshi is that spirit in us which restricts us to
the use and service of our immediate surroundings to
the exclusion of the more remote. Thus, as for religion, in order to satisfy the requirements of the definition, I must restrict myself to my ancestral religion.
That is, the use of my immediate religious surrounding. If I find it defective, I should serve it by purging
it of its defects. In the domain of politics I should
make use of the indigenous institutions and serve
them by curing them of their proved defects. In that
of economics I should use only things that are produced by my immediate neighbours and serve those
industries by making them efficient and complete
where they might be found wanting. It is suggested

that such Swadeshi, if reduced to practice, will lead
to the millennium. . . .

Let us briefly examine the three branches of Swadeshi as sketched above. Hinduism has become a con-
servative religion and, therefore, a mighty force
because of the Swadeshi spirit underlying it. It is the
most tolerant because it is non-proselytizing, and it
is as capable of expansion today as it has been found
to be in the past. It has succeeded not in driving
out, as I think it has been erroneously held, but in
absorbing Buddhism. By reason of the Swadeshi
spirit, a Hindu refuses to change his religion, not
necessarily because he considers it to be the best,
but because he knows that he can complement it by
introducing reforms. And what I have said about
Hinduism is, I suppose, true of the other great faiths
of the world, only it is held that it is specially so in
the case of Hinduism. But here comes the point I
am labouring to reach. If there is any substance in
what I have said, will not the great missionary bodies
of India, to whom she owes a deep debt of gratitude
for what they have done and are doing, do still better
and serve the spirit of Christianity better by dropping
the goal of proselytizing while continuing their
philanthropic work?

Following out the Swadeshi spirit, I observe the
indigenous institutions, and the village Panchayats
hold me. India is really a republican country, and it
is because it is that, that it has survived every shock
hitherto delivered. Princes and potentates, whether
they were Indian born or foreigners, have hardly
touched the vast masses except for collecting revenue. The latter in their turn seem to have rendered
unto Caesar what was Caesar's and for the rest have

done much as they have liked. The vast organization of caste answered not only to the religious wants
of the community but it answered to its political
needs. The villagers managed their internal affairs
through the caste system and through it they dealt
with any oppression from the ruling power or
powers. It is not possible to deny the organizing
ability of a nation that was capable of producing
from the caste system its wonderful power of organization. One has but to attend the great Kumbha
Mela at Hardwar . . . to know how skilful that
organization must have been which, without any
seeming effort, was able effectively to cater for more
than a million pilgrims. Yet it is the fashion to say
that we lack organizing ability. This is true, I fear,
to a certain extent, of those who have been nurtured
in the new traditions.

We have laboured under a terrible handicap
owing to an almost fatal departure from the Swadeshi
spirit. We, the educated classes, have received our
education through a foreign tongue. We have, therefore, not reacted upon the masses. We want to represent the masses, but we fail. They recognize us
not much more than they recognize the English
officers. Their hearts are an open book to neither.
Their aspirations are not ours. Hence there is a break.
And you witness not in reality failure to organize but
want of correspondence between the representatives
and the represented. If during the last fifty years we
had been educated through the vernaculars, our
elders and our servants and our neighbours would
have partaken of our knowledge; the discoveries of
a Bose or a Ray would have been household treasures
as are the Ramayana and the Mahabharata. As it is,

so far as the masses are concerned, those great discoveries might as well have been made by foreigners.
Had instruction in all the branches of learning been
given through the vernaculars, I make bold to say
that they would have been enriched wonderfully.
The question of village sanitation etc. would have
been solved long ago. The village Panchayats would
be now a living force in a special way, and India
would almost be enjoying self-government suited to
her requirements, and would have been spared the
humiliating spectacle of organized assassination on
her sacred soil. It is not too late to mend.

And now for the last division of Swadeshi. Much
of the deep poverty of the masses is due to the ruinous
departure from Swadeshi in the economic and industrial life. If not one article of commerce had been
brought from outside India, she would be today a
land flowing with milk and honey. But that was not
to be. We were greedy and so was England. The
connection between England and India was based
clearly upon an error. But she does not remain in
India in error. It is her declared policy that India is
to be held in trust for her people. If this be true,
Lancashire must stand aside. And if the Swadeshi
doctrine is a sound doctrine, Lancashire can stand
aside without hurt, though it may sustain a shock
for the time being. I think of Swadeshi not as a boycott movement undertaken by way of revenge. I conceive it as a religious principle to be followed by all.
I am no economist, but I have read some treatises
which show that England could easily become a self-
sustained country, growing all the produce she needs.
This may be an utterly ridiculous proposition, and
perhaps the best proof that it cannot be true, is that

England is one of the largest importers in the world. But India cannot live for Lancashire or any other country before she is able to live for herself. And she can live for herself only if she produces and is helped to produce everything for her requirements within her own borders. She need not be, she ought not be, drawn into the vortex of mad and ruinous competition which breeds fratricide, jealousy and many other evils. But who is to stop her great millionaires from entering into the world competition? Certainly not legislation. Force of public opinion and proper education, however, can do a great deal in the desired direction. The handloom industry is in a dying condition. I took special care during my wanderings. . . to see as many weavers as possible, and my heart ached to find how they had lost, how families had retired from this once flourishing and honourable occupation.

If we follow the Swadeshi doctrine, it would be your duty and mine to find out neighbours who can supply our wants and to teach them to supply them where they do not know how to proceed, assuming that there are neighbours who are in want of healthy occupation. Then every village of India will almost be a self-supporting and self-contained unit, exchanging only such necessary commodities with other villages as are not locally producible. This may all sound nonsensical. Well, India is a country of nonsense. It is nonsensical to parch one's throat with thirst when a kindly Mohammedan is ready to offer pure water to drink. And yet thousands of Hindus would rather die of thirst than drink water from a Mohammedan household. These nonsensical men can also, once they are convinced that

their religion demands that they should wear garments manufactured in India only and eat food
only grown in India, decline to wear any other clothing or eat any other food.

There is a verse in the Bhagavadgita which,
freely rendered, means masses follow the classes.
It is easy to undo the evil if the thinking portion of
the community were to take the Swadeshi vow, even
though it may for a time cause considerable in-
convenience. I hate legislative interference in any
department of life. At best it is the lesser evil. But I
would tolerate, welcome—indeed, plead for a stiff
protective duty upon foreign goods. Natal, a British
colony, protected its sugar by taxing the sugar that
came from another British colony, Mauritius.
England has sinned against India by forcing free
trade upon her. It may have been food for her, but
it has been poison for this country.

It has often been urged that India cannot adopt
Swadeshi in the economic life at any rate. Those who
advance this objection do not look upon Swadeshi as
a rule of life. With them it is a mere patriotic effort—
not to be made if it involved any self-denial.
Swadeshi, as defined here, is a religious discipline
to be undergone in utter disregard of the physical
discomfort it may cause to individuals. Under its spell
the deprivation of a pin or a needle, because these
are not manufactured in India, need cause no terror.
A Swadeshist will learn to do without hundreds of
things which today he considers necessary. Moreover, those who dismiss Swadeshi from their minds
by arguing the impossible, forget that Swadeshi,
after all, is a goal to be reached by steady effort.

And we would be making for the goal even if we confined Swadeshi to a given set of articles allowing ourselves as a temporary measure to use such things as might not be procurable in the country.

There now remains for me to consider one more objection that has been raised against Swadeshi. The objectors consider it to be a most selfish doctrine without any warrant in the civilized code of morality. With them to practise Swadeshi is to revert to barbarism. I cannot enter into a detailed analysis of the proposition. But I would urge that Swadeshi is the only doctrine consistent with the law of humility and love. It is arrogance to think of launching out to serve the whole of India when I am hardly able to serve even my own family. It were better to concentrate my effort upon the family and consider that through them I was serving the whole nation and, if you will, the whole of humanity. This is humility and it is love. The motive will determine the quality of the act. I may serve my family regardless of the sufferings I may cause to others. As, for instance, I may accept an employment which enables me to extort money from people. I enrich myself thereby and then satisfy many unlawful demands of the family. Here I am neither serving the family nor the State. Or I may recognize that God has given me hands and feet only to work with for my sustenance and for that of those who may be dependent upon me. I would then at once simplify my life and that of those whom I can directly reach. In this instance I would have served the family without causing injury to anyone else. Supposing that every one followed this mode of life, we should have at once an ideal state. All will not reach that state at the same time. But those of us who, realizing its truth, enforce it in practice, will clearly anticipate and accelerate the coming of that happy day. Under this plan of life, in seeming to serve India to the exclusion of every other country, I do not harm any other country. My patriotism is both exclusive and inclusive. It is exclusive in the sense that in all humility I confine my attention to the land of my birth, but is inclusive in the sense that my service is not of a competitive or antagonistic nature. *Sic utere tuo ut alienum non laedas* is not merely a legal maxim, but it is a grand doctrine of life. It is the key to a proper practice of Ahimsa or love. *1*

Even Swadeshi like any other good thing can be ridden to death if it is made a fetish. That is a danger that must be guarded against. To reject foreign manufactures, merely because they are foreign and to go on wasting national time and money in the promotion in one's country of manufactures for which it is not suited, would be criminal folly and a negation of the Swadeshi spirit. A true votary of Swadeshi will not harbour ill-will towards a foreigner and not be actuated by antagonism towards anybody on the earth. Swadeshi is not a cult of hatred. It is a doctrine of selfless service that has its roots in the purest Ahimsa, i. e., love. *2*

CHAPTER 11

SELF-SUFFICIENCY AND CO-OPERATION

Truth and non-violence form the foundation of the order of my conception. Our first duty is that we should not be a burden on society, i.e., we should be self-dependent. From this point of view self-sufficiency itself is a kind of service. After becoming self-sufficient we shall use our spare time for the service of others. If all become self-sufficient none will be in trouble. In such a state of affairs there would be no need of serving anybody. But we have not yet reached that stage and therefore we have to think of social service. Even if we succeed in realizing self-sufficiency completely, man being a social being, we will have to accept service in some form or other. That is, man is as much self-dependent as inter-dependent. When dependence becomes necessary in order to keep society in good order it is no longer dependence, but becomes co-operation. There is sweetness in co-operation; there is no one weak or strong among those who co-operate. Each is equal to the other. There is the feeling of helplessness in dependency. Members of a family are as much self-dependent as inter-dependent. There is no feeling of either mine or thine. They are all co-operators. So also when we take a society, a nation or the whole of mankind as a family all men become co-operators. If we can conceive a picture of such co-operation we shall find that there would be no need of support from the lifeless machine. Instead of making the greatest use of machinery we shall be able to do with the least use thereof and therein lies the real security and self-protection of society. *1*

My idea of self-sufficiency is that villages must be self-sufficient in regard to food, cloth and other basic necessities. But even this can be overdone. Therefore you must grasp my idea properly. Self-sufficiency does not mean narrowness. To be self-sufficient is not to be altogether self-contained. In no circumstances would we be able to produce all the things we need. So though our aim is complete self-sufficiency, we shall have to get from outside the village what we cannot produce in the village; we shall have to produce more of what we can in order thereby to obtain in exchange what we are unable to produce. *2*

The ideal no doubt is for every family to grow, spin, weave and wear its own cotton, just as it is for every family to own land and grow its own corn, cook and eat it. *3*

As for food, India has plenty of fertile land, there is enough water and no dearth of man power. . . . The public should be educated to become self-reliant. Once they know that they have got to stand on their own legs, it would electrify the atmosphere.

India produces more cotton than she requires for her wants. People should spin and weave themselves. People should produce their own Khadi. Once the people begin to produce their own food and cloth, it would change their entire outlook. *4*

Self-sufficiency is a big word. . . . Villages will be swept away, if they are not self-sufficient as to their primary wants and self-reliant as to their

protection against internal disruption by dissen-
sions and disease and external danger from thieves
and dacoits. Self-sufficiency, therefore, means all
the cotton processes and growing of seasonal food
crops and fodder for cattle. Unless this is done there
will be starvation. And self-reliance means corporate
organization ensuring adjustment of internal differences through arbitration by the wise men of villages and cleanliness by corporate attention to
sanitation and common diseases. No mere individual
effort is going to suffice. And above all, villagers must
be taught to feel their own strength by combined
effort to make their villages proof against thieves
and dacoits. This is best done by corporate non-
violence. But if the way to non-violence does not
seem clear to workers, they will not hesitate to organize corporate defence through violence. 5

Self-sufficient Khadi will never succeed without cotton being grown by spinners themselves or
practically in every village. It means decentralization of cotton cultivation so far at least as self-
sufficient Khadi is concerned. For this we shall need
a census of the villages served. For not every spinner
or weaver has a plot (ever so tiny) of land, where he
or she can grow cotton. Self-sufficient Khadi is a
proposition for which alone can the existence of the
A.I.S.A. be justified. It is a field as yet untouched by
it on any scale worth mentioning. 6

We can but serve that part of God's creation
which is nearest and best known to us. We can
start with our next-door neighbour. We should not
be content with keeping our courtyard clean, we
should see that our neighbour's courtyard is also
clean. We may serve our family, but may not sacrifice

the village for the sake of the family. Our own honour lies in the preservation of that of our own village. But we must each of us understand our own limitations. Our capacity for service is automatically limited by our knowledge of the world in which we live. But let me put it in the simplest possible language. Let us think less of ourselves than of our next-door neighbour. Dumping the refuse of our court-yard into that of our neighbour is no service of humanity, but disservice. Let us start with the service of our neighbour. 7

In regard to agriculture, we must do our utmost to prevent further fragmentation of land, and to encourage people to take to co-operative farming. 8

A village may grow cotton for itself in co-opera-tion. If this is done, it is simple enough to see that no imported cloth can beat cloth thus produced locally, either in cost or durability. The process induces the greatest conservation of energy. 9

Let us not also forget that it is man's social nature which distinguishes him from the brute creation. If it is his privilege to be independent it is equally his duty to be interdependent. Only an arrogant man will claim to be independent of everybody else and be self-contained. . . . It will be possible to reconstruct our villages so that the villages collectively, not the villagers individually, will become self-contained, so far as their clothing requirements are concerned. 10

In speaking to a co-operative society in Madras last year, I said that through hand-spinning I was trying to found the largest co-operative society known to the world. This is not an untrue claim. It may be ambitious. It is not untrue because hand-spinning cannot ·serve the purpose for which it is intended unless millions actually co-operate in it.

Take the working of any typical centre. At the central office is collected seed cotton for spinners. The cotton is ginned by ginners perhaps at the centres. It is distributed then among carders who re-deliver it in the shape of slivers. These are now ready to be distributed among the spinners who bring their yarn from week to week and take away fresh slivers and their wages in return. The yarn thus received is given to weavers to weave and received back for sale in the shape of khaddar. This latter must now be sold to the weavers—the general public. Thus the central office has to be in constant living human touch with a very large number of people irrespective of caste, colour or creed. For the centre has no dividends to make, has no exclusive care but the care of the most needy. The centre to be useful must keep itself clean in every sense of the term. The bond between it and the component parts of the vast organization is purely spiritual or moral. A spinning centre, therefore, is a co-operative society whose members are ginners, carders, spinners, weavers and buyers—all tied together by a common bond, mutual good-will and service. *11*

The secret of successful co-operative effort is that the members must be honest and know the great merit of co-operation and it must have a definite progressive goal. Thus holding a certain sum of money in co-operation for the sake of making more money by charging exorbitant rates of interest is a bad goal. But co-operative 'farming or dairying is undoubtedly a good goal promoting national interests. Such instances can be multiplied. I wonder

what these numerous . . . societies are. Have
they honest inspectors who know their work? It
may be mentioned that such movements have often
proved disastrous when management has been dis-
honest and the goal questionable. *12*

CHAPTER 12

PANCHAYAT RAJ

Panchayats in Pre-independence Days

Panchayat has an ancient flavour; it is a good
word. It literally means an assembly of five elected
by villagers. It represents the system, by which the
innumerable village republics of India were governed.
But the British Government, by its ruthlessly thorough
method of revenue collection, almost destroyed these
ancient republics, which could not stand the shock
of this revenue collection. Congressmen are now making
a crude attempt to revive the system by giving village
elders civil and criminal jurisdiction. The attempt
was first made in 1921. It failed. It is being made
again, and it will fail if it is not systematically and
decently, I will not say, scientifically, tried.

It was reported to me in Nainital, that in certain
places in the U.P., even criminal cases like rape were
tried by the so-called Panchayats. I heard of some
fantastic judgments pronounced by ignorant or
interested Panchayats. This is all bad if it is true.
Irregular Panchayats are bound to fall to pieces under
their own unsupportable weight, I suggest, therefore,
the following rules for the guidance of village workers:

1. No Panchayat should be set up without the written sanction of a Provincial Congress Committee;

2. A Panchayat should in the first instance be elected by a public meeting called for the purpose by beat of drums;

3. It should be recommended by the Tahsil Committee;

4. Such Panchayat should have no criminal jurisdiction;

5. It may try civil suits if the parties to them refer their disputes to the Panchayat;

6. No one should be compelled to refer any matter to the Panchayat;

7. No Panchayat should have any authority to impose fines, the only sanction behind its civil decrees being its moral authority, strict impartiality and the willing obedience of the parties concerned;

8. There should be no social or other boycott for the time being;

9. Every Panchayat will be expected to attend to:

    (a) The education of boys and girls in its village;

    (b) Its sanitation;

    (c) Its medical needs;

    (d) The upkeep and cleanliness of village wells or ponds;

    (e) The uplift of and the daily wants of the so-called untouchables.

10. A Panchayat that fails without just cause to attend to the requirements mentioned in clause 9 within six months of its election, or fails otherwise to retain the goodwill of the villagers, or stands self-

condemned for any other cause, appearing sufficient to the Provincial Congress Committee, may be disbanded and another elected in its place.

The disability to impose fines or social boycott is a necessity of the case in the initial stages; social boycott in villages has been found to be a dangerous weapon in the hands of ignorant or unscrupulous men. Imposition of fines too may lead to mischief and defeat the very end in view. Where a Panchayat is really popular and increases its popularity by the constructive work of the kind suggested in clause 9, it will find its judgments and authority respected by reason of its moral prestige. And that surely is the greatest sanction anyone can possess and of which one cannot be deprived. *1*

Panchayats in Independent India

Independence must mean that of the people of India, not of those who are today ruling over them. The rulers should depend on the will of those who are under their heels. Thus, they have to be servants of the people, ready to do their will.

Independence must begin at the bottom. Thus, every village will be a republic or Panchayat having full powers. It follows, therefore, that every village has to be self-sustained and capable of managing its affairs even to the extent of defending itself against the whole world. It will be trained and prepared to perish in the attempt to defend itself against any onslaught from without. Thus, ultimately, it is the individual who is the unit. This does not exclude dependence on and willing help from neighbours or from the world. It will be free and voluntary play of mutual forces. Such a society is necessarily highly cultured in which every man and woman knows what he or she wants and, what is more, knows that no one should want anything that others cannot have with equal labour.

This society must naturally be based on truth and non-violence which, in my opinion, are not possible without a living belief in God meaning a Self-existent, All-knowing Living Force which inheres every other force known to the world and which depends on none and which will live when all other forces may conceivably perish or cease to act. I am unable to account for my life without belief in this All-embracing Living Force.

In this structure composed of innumerable villages there will be ever-widening, never ascending circles. Life will not be a pyramid with the apex sustained by the bottom. But it will be an oceanic circle whose centre will be the individual always ready to perish for the village, the latter ready to perish for the circle of villages, till at last the whole becomes one life composed of individuals, never aggressive in their arrogance but ever humble, sharing the majesty of the oceanic circle of which they are integral units.

Therefore, the outermost circumference will not wield power to crush the inner circle but give strength to all within and derive its own from the centre. I may be taunted with the retort that this is all utopian and therefore not worth a single thought. If Euclid's point, though incapable of being drawn by human agency, has an imperishable value, my picture has its own for mankind to live. Let India live for this true picture, though never realizable in its completeness. We must have a proper picture of what we want before we can have something approaching it. If there ever is to be a republic of every village in India, then I claim verity for my picture in which the last is equal to the first, or in other words, none is to be the first and none the last.

In this picture every religion has its full and equal place. We are all leaves of a majestic tree whose trunk cannot be shaken off its roots which are deep down in the bowels of the earth. The mightiest of winds cannot move it.

In this there is no room for machines that would displace human labour and that would concentrate power in a few hands. Labour has its unique place in a cultural human family. Every machine that helps every individual has a place. But I must confess that I have never sat down to think out what that machine can be. I have thought of Singer's sewing machine. But even that is perfunctory. I do not need it to fill in my picture. 2

What should we do then? If we would see our dream of Panchayat Raj, i.e. true democracy realized, we would regard the humblest and lowest Indian as being equally the ruler of India with the tallest in the land. This presupposes that all are pure or will become pure if they are not. And purity must go hand-in-hand with wisdom. No one would then harbour any distinction between community and community, caste and out-caste. Everybody would regard all as equal with oneself and hold them together in the silken net of love. No one would regard another as untouchable. We would hold as equal the toiling labourer and the rich capitalist. Everybody would know how to earn an honest living by the sweat of one's brow and make no distinction between intellectual and physical labour. To hasten this consummation, we would voluntarily turn ourselves into scavengers. No one who has wisdom will ever touch opium, liquor or any intoxicants. Everybody would observe Swadeshi as the rule of life and regard every woman, not being his wife, as his mother, sister or daughter according to her age, never lust after her in his heart. He would be ready to lay down his life when occasion demands it, never want to take another's life. If he is a Sikh in terms of the commandment of the Gurus he would have the heroic courage to stand single-handed and alone, without yielding an inch of ground against the "one lakh and a quarter" enjoined by them. Needless to say, such a son of India will not want to be told what his duty in the present hour is. 3

Duties of the Panchayat

Distinguished travellers from the world came to India in the days of yore from China and other countries. They came in quest of knowledge and put up with great hardships in travelling. They had reported that in India there was no theft, people were honest and industrious. They needed no locks for their doors. In those days there was no multiplicity of castes as at present. It is the function of Panchayats to revive honesty and industry. It is the function of the Panchayats to teach the villagers to avoid disputes, if they have to settle them. That would ensure speedy justice without any expenditure. They would need neither the police nor the military.

Then the Panchayat should see to cattle improvement. They should show steady increase in the milk yield. Our cattle have become a burden on the land for want of care. It is gross ignorance to blame the

Muslims for cow slaughter. It is the Hindus who kill the cattle by inches through ill-treatment. Slow death by torture is far worse than outright killing.

The Panchayat should also see to an increase in the quantity of foodstuff grown in their village. That is to be accomplished by properly manuring the soil. The Compost Conference recently held in Delhi under the inspiration of Shrimati Mirabehn has told them how the excreta of animals and human beings mixed with rubbish can be turned into valuable manure. This manure increases the fertility of the soil. Then they must see to the cleanliness of their village and its inhabitants. They must be clean and healthy in body and mind.

There should be no cinema house. People say that the cinema can be a potent means of education. That might come true some day, but at the moment I see how much harm the cinema is doing. They have their indigenous games. They should banish intoxicating drinks and drugs from their midst. They should eradicate untouchability if there is any trace of it still left in their village. The Hindus, Muslims, Sikhs, Parsis and Christians should all live as brothers and sisters. If they achieve all I have mentioned, they would demonstrate real independence and people from all over India would come to see their model village and take inspiration from it. 4

CHAPTER 13

NAI TALIM

I

Nai Talim was popularly and correctly described as education through handicrafts. This was part of the truth. The root of this new education went much deeper. It lay in the application of truth and love in every variety of human activity, whether in individual life or a corporate one. The notion of education through handicraft rose from the contemplation of truth and love permeating life's activities. Love required that true education should be easily accessible to all and should be of use to every villager in his daily life. Such education was not derived from nor did it depend upon books. It had no relation to sectional religion. If it could be called religious, it was universal religion from which all sectional religions were derived. Therefore, it was learnt from the Book of Life which cost nothing and which could not be taken away from one by any force on earth. *1*

I hold that true education of the intellect can only come through a proper exercise and training of the bodily organs, e.g. hands, feet, eyes, ears, nose, etc. In other words an intelligent use of the bodily organs in a child provides the best and quickest way of developing his intellect. But unless the development of the mind and body goes hand in hand with a corresponding awakening of the soul, the former alone would prove to be a poor lop-sided affair. By spiritual training I mean education of the heart. A proper and all-round development of the mind, therefore, can take place only when it proceeds *pari passu* with the education of the physical and spiritual faculties of the child. They constitute an indivisible whole. According to this theory, therefore, it would be a gross fallacy to suppose that they can be developed piecemeal or independently of one another.

The baneful effects of absence of proper co-ordination and harmony among the various faculties of body, mind and soul respectively are obvious. They are all around us; only we have lost perception of them owing to our present perverse associations. Take the case of our village folk. From their childhood upward they toil and labour in their fields from morning till night like their cattle in the midst of whom they live. Their existence is a weary endless round of mechanical drudgery unrelieved by a spark of intelligence or higher graces of life. Deprived of all scope for developing their mind and soul, they have sunk to the level of the beast. Life to them is a sorry bungle which they muddle through anyhow. On the other hand what goes by the name of education in our schools and colleges in the cities today is in reality only intellectual dissipation. Intellectual training is there looked upon as something altogether unrelated to manual or physical work. But since the body must have some sort of physical exercise to keep it in health, they vainly try to attain that end by means of artificial and otherwise barren system of physical culture which would be ridiculous beyond words if the result was not so tragic. The young man who emerges from this system can in no way compete in physical endurance with an ordinary labourer. The slightest physical exertion gives him a headache; a mild exposure to the sun is enough to cause him giddiness. And what is more, all this is looked upon as quite 'natural'. As for the faculties of the heart, they are simply allowed to run to seed or to grow anyhow in a wild undisciplined manner. The result is moral and spiritual anarchy. And it is regarded as something laudable!!

As against this, take the case of a child in whom the education of the heart is attended to from the very beginning. Supposing he is set to some useful occupation like spinning, carpentry, agriculture, etc., for his education and in that connection is given a thorough comprehensive knowledge relating to the theory of the various operations that he is to perform and the use and construction of the tools that he would be wielding. He would not only develop a fine healthy body but also a sound, vigorous intellect that is not merely academic but is firmly rooted in and is tested from day to day by experience. His intellectual education would include a knowledge of mathematics and the various sciences that are useful for an intelligent and efficient exercise of his avocation. If to this is added literature by way of recreation, it would give him a perfect well-balanced, all-round education in which the intellect, the body and the spirit have all full play and develop together into a natural, harmonious whole. Man is neither mere intellect, nor the gross animal body, nor the heart or soul alone. A proper and harmonious combination of all the three is required for the making of the whole man and constitutes the true economics of education. [2]

If we want to impart education best suited to the needs of villagers, we should take the Vidyapith to the villages. We should convert it into a training school in order that we might be able to give practical training to teachers in terms of the needs of villagers. You cannot instruct the teachers in the needs of villagers through a training school in a city. Nor can you so interest them in the condition of villages. To interest city-dwellers in villages and make them live in them is no easy task. I am finding daily confirmation of this in Segaon. I cannot give you the assurance that our year's stay in Segaon has made of us villagers or that we have become one with them for the common good.

Then as to primary education, my confirmed opinion is that the commencement of training by teaching the alphabet and reading and writing hampers their intellectual growth. I would not teach them the alphabet till they have had an elementary knowledge of history, geography, mental arithmetic and the art (say) of spinning. Through these three I should develop their intelligence. Question may be asked how intelligence can be developed through the *takli* or the spinning wheel. It can to a marvellous degree if it is not taught merely mechanically. When you tell a child the reason for each process, when you explain the mechanism of the *takli* or the wheel, when you give him the history of cotton and its connection with civilization itself and take him to the village field where it is grown, and teach him to count the rounds he spins and the method of finding the evenness and strength of his yarn, you hold his interest and simultaneously train his hands, his eyes and his mind. I should give six months to this preliminary training. The child is probably now ready for learning how to read the alphabet, and when he is able to do so rapidly, he is ready to learn simple drawing, and when he has learnt to draw geometrical figures and the figures of the birds etc., he will draw, not scrawl, the figures of the alphabet. I can recall the days of my childhood when I was being taught the alphabet. I know what a drag it was. Nobody cared why my intellect was rusting. I consider writing as a fine art. We kill it by imposing the alphabet on little children and making it the beginning of learning. Thus we do violence to the art of writing and stunt the growth of the child when we seek to teach him the alphabet before its time. 3

As to the necessity and value of regarding the teaching of village handicrafts as the pivot and centre of education I have no manner of doubt. The method adopted in the institutions in India I do not call education, i.e. drawing out the best in man, but a debauchery of the mind. It informs the mind anyhow, whereas the method of training the mind through village handicrafts from the beginning as the central fact would promote the real, disciplined development of the mind resulting in conservation of the intellectual energy and indirectly also the spiritual. 4

In my scheme of things the hand will handle tools before it draws or traces the writing. The eyes will read the pictures of letters and words as they will know other things in life, the ears will catch the names and meanings of things and sentences. The whole training will be natural, responsive, and therefore the quickest and the cheapest in the land. The children of my school will therefore read much more quickly than they will write. And when they write they will not produce daubs as I do even now (thanks to my teachers) but they will trace correct letters even as they will trace correct figures of the objects they may see. If the schools of my conception ever come into being, I make bold to say that they will vie with the most advanced schools in quickness, so far as reading is concerned, and even writing if it is common ground that the writing must be correct and not incorrect as now is in the vast majority of cases. 5

The course of primary education should be extended at least to seven years and should include the general knowledge gained up to the matriculation standard less English and plus a substantial vocation.

For the all-round development of boys and girls all training should so far as possible be given through a profit-yielding vocation. In other words vocations should serve a double purpose—to enable the pupils to pay for his tuition through the products of his labour and at the same time to develop the whole man or woman in him or her through the vocation learnt at school.

Land, buildings and equipment are not intended to be covered by the proceeds of the pupil's labour.

All the processes of cotton, wool and silk, commencing from gathering, cleaning, ginning (in the case of cotton), carding, spinning, dyeing, sizing, warp-making, double-twisting, designing and weaving, embroidery, tailoring, paper-making, cutting, book-binding, cabinet-making, toy-making, gur-making are undoubted occupations that can easily be learnt and handled without much capital outlay.

This primary education should equip boys and girls to earn their bread by the State guaranteeing employment in the vocations learnt or by buying their manufactures at prices fixed by the State. 6

But as a nation we are so backward in education that we cannot hope to fulfil our obligations to the nation in this respect in the given time during this generation, if the programme is to depend on money. I have therefore made bold, even at the risk of losing all reputation for constructive ability, to suggest that education should be self-supporting. By education I mean an all-round drawing out of the best in child and man—body, mind and spirit. Literacy is not the end of education nor even the beginning. It is only one of the means whereby man and woman can be educated. Literacy in itself is no education. I would therefore begin the child's education by teaching it a useful handicraft and enabling it to produce from the moment it begins its training. Thus every school can be made self-supporting, the condition being that the State takes over the manufactures of these schools.

I hold that the highest development of the mind and the soul is possible under such a system of education. Only every handicraft has to be taught not merely mechanically as is done today but scientifically, i.e. the child should know the why and the wherefore of every process. I am not writing this without some confidence, because it has the backing of experience. This method is being adopted more or less completely wherever spinning is being taught to workers. I have myself taught sandal-making and even spinning on these lines with good results. This method does not exclude a knowledge of history and geography. But I find that this is best taught by transmitting such general information by word of mouth. One imparts ten times as much in this manner as by reading and writing. The signs of the alphabet may be taught later when the pupil has learnt to distinguish the wheat from the chaff and when he has somewhat developed his or her tastes. This is a revolutionary proposal but it saves immense labour and enables a student to acquire in one year what he may take much longer to learn. This means all-round economy. Of course the pupil learns mathematics whilst he is learning his handicraft.

I attach the greatest importance to primary education which according to my conception should be equal to the present matriculation less English. If all the collegians were all of a sudden to forget their knowledge, the loss sustained by the sudden lapse of the memory of say a few lakhs of collegians would be as nothing compared to the loss that the nation has sustained and is sustaining through the ocean of darkness that surrounds three hundred millions. The measure of illiteracy is no adequate measure of the prevailing ignorance among the millions of villagers.

I would revolutionize college education and relate it to national necessities. There would be degrees for mechanical and other engineers. They would be attached to the different industries which should pay for the training of the graduates they need. Thus the Tatas would be expected to run a college for training engineers under the supervision of the State, the mill associations would run among them a college for training graduates whom they need. Similarly for the other industries that may be named. Commerce will have its college. There remain arts, medicine and agriculture. Several private arts colleges are today self-supporting. The State would, therefore, cease to run its own. Medical colleges would be attached to certified hospitals. As they are popular among moneyed men they may be expected by voluntary contributions to support medical colleges. And agricultural colleges to be worthy of the name must be self-supporting. I have a painful experience of some agricultural graduates. Their knowledge is superficial. They lack practical experience. But if they had their apprenticeship on farms which are self-sustained and answer the requirements of the country, they would not have to gain experience after getting their degrees and at the expense of their employers. 7

Given the right kind of teachers, our children will be taught the dignity of labour and learn to regard it as an integral part and a means of their intellectual growth, and to realize that it is patriotic to pay for their training through their labour. The core of my suggestion is that handicrafts are to be taught, not merely for productive works, but for developing the intellect of the pupils. Surely, if the State takes charge of the children between seven and fourteen, and trains their bodies and minds through productive labour, the public schools must be frauds and teachers idiots, if they cannot become self-supporting. 8

We have up to now concentrated on stuffing children's minds with all kinds of information, without ever thinking of stimulating and developing them. Let us now cry a halt and concentrate on educating the child properly through manual work, not as a side activity, but as the prime means of intellectual training. 9

In the schools I advocate, boys have all that boys learn in high schools less English but plus drill, music, drawing, and, of course, a vocation. 10

I am a firm believer in the principle of free and compulsory primary education for India. I also hold that we shall realize this only by teaching the children a useful vocation and utilizing it as a means for cultivating their mental, physical and spiritual faculties. Let no one consider these economic calculations in connection with education as sordid, or out of place. There is nothing essentially sordid about economic calculations. True economics never militates against the highest ethical standard, just as all true ethics to be worth its name must at the same time be also good economics. *11*

What kind of vocations are the fittest for being taught to children in urban schools? There is no hard and fast rule about it. But my reply is clear. I want to resuscitate the villages of India. Today our villages have become a mere appendage to the cities. They exist, as it were, to be exploited by the latter and depend on the latter's sufferance. This is unnatural. It is only when the cities realize the duty of making an adequate return to the villages for the strength and sustenance which they derive from them, instead of selfishly exploiting them, that a healthy and moral relationship between the two will spring up. And if the city children are to play their part in this great and noble work of social reconstruction, the vocations through which they are to receive their education ought to be directly related to the requirements of the villages. So far as I can see the various processes of cotton manufacture from ginning and cleaning of cotton to the spinning of yarn, answer this test as nothing else does. Even today cotton is grown in the villages and is ginned and spun and converted into cloth in the cities. But the chain of processes which cotton undergoes in the mills from the beginning to the end constitutes a huge tragedy of waste in men, materials and mechanical power.

My plan to impart primary education through the medium of village handicrafts like spinning and carding etc. is thus conceived as the spear-head of a silent social revolution fraught with the most far-reaching consequences. It will provide a healthy and moral basis of relationship between the city and the village and thus go a long way toward eradicating some of the worst evils of the present social insecurity and poisoned relationship between the classes. It will check the progressive decay of our villages and lay the foundation of a juster social order in which there is no unnatural division between the 'haves' and 'have-nots' and everybody is assured of a living wage and the right to freedom. And all this would be accomplished without the horrors of a bloody class war or a colossal capital expenditure such as would be involved in the mechanization of a vast continent like India. Nor would it entail a helpless dependence on foreign imported machinery or technical skill. Lastly, by obviating the necessity for highly specialized talent, it would place the destiny of the masses, as it were, in their own hands. But who will bell the cat? Will the city-folk listen to me at all? Or, will mine remain a mere cry in the wilderness? Replies to these and similar questions will depend more on lovers of education living in cities than on me. 12

If such education is given, the direct result will be that it will be self-supporting. But the test of success is not its self-supporting character, but that the whole man has been drawn out through the teaching of the handicraft in a scientific manner. In fact I would reject a teacher who would promise to make it self-supporting under any circumstances. The self-supporting part will be the logical corollary of the fact that the pupil has learnt the use of every one of his faculties. If a boy who works at a handicraft for three hours a day will surely earn his keep, how much more a boy who adds to the work a development of his mind and soul!.13

This basic education has grown out of the atmosphere surrounding us in the country and is in response to it. It is, therefore, designed to cope with that atmosphere. This atmosphere pervades India's seven hundred thousand villages and its millions of inhabitants. Forget them and you forget India. India is not to be found in her cities. It is in her innumerable villages.

The following are the fundamentals of basic education:

1. All education to be true must be self-supporting, that is to say, in the end it will pay its expenses excepting the capital which will remain intact.

2. In it the cunning of the hand will be utilized even up to the final stage, that is to say, hands of the pupils will be skilfully working at some industry for some period during the day.

3. All education must be imparted through the medium of the provincial language.

4. In this there is no room for giving sectional religious training. Fundamental universal ethics will have full scope.

5. This education, whether it is confined to children or adults, male or female, will find its way to the homes of the pupils.

6. Since millions of students receiving this education will consider themselves as of the whole of India, they must learn an inter-provincial language. This common inter-provincial speech can only be Hindustani written in Nagari or Urdu script. Therefore, pupils have to master both the scripts. *14*

II

All instruction must be linked with some basic craft. When you are imparting knowledge to a child of 7 or 10 through the medium of an industry, you should, to begin with, exclude all those subjects which cannot be linked with the craft. By doing so from day to day you will discover ways and means of linking with the craft many things which you had excluded in the beginning. You will save your own energy and the pupil's if you follow this process of exclusion to begin with. We have today no books to go by, no precedents to guide us. Therefore we have to go slow. The main thing is that the teacher should retain his freshness of mind. If you come across something that you cannot correlate with the craft, do not fret over it and get disheartened. Leave it, and go ahead with the subjects that you can correlate. May be another teacher will hit upon the right way and show how it can be correlated. And when you have pooled the experience of many, you will have books to guide you, so that the work of those who follow you will become easier.

How long, you will ask, are we to go on with this process of exclusion. My reply is, for the whole life-time. At the end you will find that you have included many things that you have excluded at first, that practically all that was worth including has been included, and whatever you have been obliged to exclude till the end was something very superficial that deserved exclusion. This has been my experience of life. I would not have been able to do many things that I have done if I had not excluded an equal number.

Our education has got to be revolutionized. The brain must be educated through the hand. If I were a poet, I could write poetry on the possibilities of the five fingers. Why should you think that the mind is everything and the hands and feet nothing? Those who do not train their hands, who go through the ordinary rut of education, lack 'music' in their life. All their faculties are not trained. Mere book knowledge does not interest the child so as to hold his attention fully. The brain gets weary of mere words, and the child's mind begins to wander. The hand does the things it ought not to do, the eye sees the things it ought not to see, the ear hears the things it ought not to hear, and they do not do, see, or hear, respectively, what they ought to. They are not taught to make the right choice and so their education often proves their ruin. An education which does not teach us to discriminate between good and bad, to assimilate the one and eschew the other is a misnomer.

The old idea was to add a handicraft to the ordinary curriculum of education followed in the schools. That is to say, the craft was to be taken in hand wholly separately from education. To me that seems a fatal mistake. The teacher must learn the craft and correlate his knowledge to the craft, so that he will impart all that knowledge to his pupils through the medium of the particular craft that he chooses.

Take the instance of spinning. Unless I know arithmetic I cannot report how many yards of yarn I have produced on the *takli*, or how many standard rounds it will make or what is the count of the yarn that I have spun. I must learn figures to be able to do so, and I also must learn addition and subtraction and multiplication and division. In dealing with complicated sums I shall have to use symbols and so get my algebra. Even here, I would insist on the use of Hindustani letters instead of Roman.

Take geometry next. What can be a better demonstration of a circle than the disc of the *takli*? I can teach all about the circle in this way, without even mentioning the name of Euclid.

Again, you may ask how I can teach my child geography and history through spinning. Some time ago I came across a book called *Cotton—The Story of Mankind*. It thrilled me. It read like a romance. It began with the history of ancient times, how and when cotton was first grown, the stages of its development, the cotton trade between the different countries and so on. As I mention the different countries to the child, I shall naturally tell him something about the history and geography of these countries. Under whose reign the different commercial treaties were signed during the different periods? Why has cotton to be imported by some countries and cloth by others? Why can every country not grow the cotton it requires? That will lead me into economics and elements of agriculture. I shall teach him to know the different varieties of cotton, in what kind of soil they grow, how to grow them, from where to get them, and so on. Thus *takli* spinning leads me into the whole history of the East India Company, what brought them here, how they destroyed our spinning industry, how the economic motive that brought them to India led them later to entertain political aspirations, how it became a causative factor in the downfall of the Moghuls and the Marathas, in the establishment of the English Raj, and then again in the awakening of the masses in our times. There is thus no end to the educative possibilities of this new scheme. And how much quicker the child will learn all that, without putting an unnecessary tax on his mind and memory.

Let me further elaborate the idea. Just as a biologist, in order to become a good biologist must learn many other sciences besides biology, basic education, if it is treated as a science, takes us into interminable channels of learning. To extend the example of the *takli*, a pupil teacher, who rivets his attention not merely on the mechanical process of spinning, which of course he must master, but on the spirit of the thing, will concentrate on the *takli* and its various aspects. He will ask himself why the *takli* is made out of a brass disc and has a steel spindle. The original *takli* had its disc made anyhow. The still more primitive *takli* consisted of a wooden spindle with a disc of slate or clay. The *takli* has been developed scientifically, and there is a reason for making the disc out of brass and the spindle out of steel. He must find out that reason. Then, the teacher must ask himself why the disc has that particular diameter, no more and no less. When he has solved these questions satisfactorily and has gone into the mathematics of the thing, your pupil becomes a good engineer. The *takli* becomes his Kamadhenu—the 'cow of plenty'. There is no limit to the possibilities of knowledge that can be imparted through this medium. It will be limited only by the energy and conviction with which you work. You have been here for three weeks. You will have spent them usefully if it has enabled you to take to this scheme seriously, so that you will say to yourself, 'I shall either do or die'.

I am elaborating the instance of spinning because I know it. If I were a carpenter, I would teach my child all these things through carpentry, or through cardboard work if I were a worker in cardboard.

What we need is educationists with originality, fired with true zeal, who will think out from day to day what they are going to teach their pupils. The teacher cannot get this knowledge through musty volumes. He has to use his own faculties of observation and thinking and impart his knowledge to the children through his lips, with the help of a craft. This means a revolution in the method of teaching, a revolution in the teacher's outlook. Up till now you have been guided by inspectors' reports. You wanted to do what the inspector might like so that you might get more money yet for your institutions or higher salaries for yourselves. But the new teacher will not care for all that. He will say, 'I have done my duty by my pupil if I have made him a better man and in doing so I have used all my resources. That is enough for me.' 15

III

This education is meant to transform village children into model villagers. It is principally designed for them. The inspiration for it ·has come ·from the villages. Congressmen who want to build up the structure of Swaraj from its very foundation dare not neglect the children. Foreign rule has unconsciously, though none the less surely, begun with the children in the field of education. Primary education is a farce designed without regard to the wants of the India of the villages and ·for that matter even of the cities. Basic education links the children, whether of the cities or the villages, to all that is best and lasting in. India. It develops both the body and the mind, and keeps the child rooted to the soil with a glorious vision of the future in the realization of which he or she begins to take his or her share from the very commencement of his or her career in school. *16*

CHAPTER 14

AGRICULTURE AND CATTLE WELFARE—I

KISAN

Our villagers depend on agriculture and cattle for ploughing. I am rather ignorant in this respect for I have no personal experience. But there is not a single village where we have no agriculture or cattle. There is the buffalo, but except in Konkan and a few other places it is not much used for agriculture. Our worker will have to keep a careful eye on the cattle wealth of his village. If we cannot use this wealth properly India is doomed to disaster and we also shall perish. For these animals will then, as in the West, become an economic burden to us and we shall have no option before us save killing them. *1*

From the very beginning it has been my firm conviction that agriculture provides the only unfailing and perennial support to the people of this country. We should take it up and see how far we can go with it as basis. I would not at all mind if some of our young men serve the country by training themselves as experts in agriculture in the place of Khadi. The time has now come for us to pay attention to agriculture. Till now I believed that improvement in agriculture was impossible unless we had the administration of the State in our own hands. My views on this are now undergoing modification. I feel that we can bring about improvements even under the present conditions, so that the cultivator may be able to make some income for himself from the land even after paying his taxes. Jawaharlal says that any extra income to the peasant through the improvement of agriculture will be swallowed up under one pretext or the other by the alien Government. But I feel that even if it were so, it should not hinder us from acquiring and spreading as much knowledge about agriculture as possible. It may be that the Government will take away any additional income that may come to the villagers through improvements in agriculture. If they do, we can protest and teach the people to resist and make it clear to the Government that it cannot loot us in this manner. I therefore hold that we must hereafter find workers who will interest themselves in agriculture.

I am, therefore, thinking of ways and means of improving the condition of the people through a rehabilitation of agriculture, cattle-breeding and all other village industries. My problem will be solved, if I succeed even in half a dozen villages, for as is the part so is the whole. 2

Bread labour is a veritable blessing to one who would observe non-violence, worship truth, and make the observance of Brahmacharya a natural act. This labour can truly be related to agriculture alone. But at present at any rate, everybody is not in a position to take to it. A person can therefore spin or weave, or take up carpentry or smithery, instead of tilling the soil always regarding agriculture however to be the ideal. 3

Years ago I read a poem in which the peasant is described as the father of the world. If God is the Provider, the cultivator is His hand. What are we going to do to discharge the debt we owe to him? So long we have only lived on the sweat of his brow. We should have begun with the soil but we could not do so. The fault is partly mine.

There were people, who said that no basic reform in agriculture was possible, without political power. They dreamt in terms of industrialization of agriculture by large-scale application of steam and electricity. Trading in soil fertility for the sake of quick returns would prove to be a disastrous, short-sighted policy. It would result in virtual depletion of the soil. Good earth called for the sweat of one's brow to yield the bread of life.

People might criticize that approach as being slow and unprogressive. I did not hold out promise of dramatic results. Nevertheless, it held the key to the prosperity of both the soil and the inhabitants living on it. Healthy, nourishing food was the *alpha* and *omega* of rural economy. The bulk of a peasant's family budget goes to feed him and his family. All other things come afterwards. Let the tiller of the soil be well fed. Let him have a sufficiency of fresh, pure milk and ghee and oil, fish, eggs, and meat if he is a non-vegetarian. What would fine clothes, for instance, avail him, if he is ill nourished and under-fed? The question of drinking-water supply and other things would come next. A consideration of these questions would naturally involve such issues, as the place of plough cattle in the economy of agri-culture as against the tractor plough and power irrigation etc. and thus, bit by bit, the whole picture of rural economy would emerge before them. In this picture cities would take their natural place and not appear as unnatural, congested spots or boils on the body politic as they were today. We stand today in danger of forgetting the use of our hands. To forget how to dig the earth and tend the soil is to forget ourselves. To think that your occupation of the ministerial chair will be vindicated if you serve the cities only, would be to forget that India really resides in her 7,00,000 village units. What would it profit a man if he gained the world but lost his soul into the bargain? *4*

The moment you talk to them [the Indian pea-sants] and they begin to speak, you will find wisdom drops from their lips. Behind the crude exterior you will find a deep reservoir of spirituality. I call this culture—you will not find such a thing in the West. You try to engage an European peasant in conver-sation and you will find that he is uninterested in things spiritual. *5*

In the case of the Indian villager, an age-old culture is hidden under an encrustment of crudeness.

Take away the encrustation, remove his chronic poverty and his illiteracy and you have the finest specimen of what a cultured, cultivated, free citizen should be. 6

We have to teach them how to economize time, health and money. Lionel Curtis described our villages as dung-heaps. We have to turn them into model villages. Our village-folk do not get fresh air though they are surrounded by fresh air; they don't get fresh food though they are surrounded by the freshest foods. I am talking like a missionary in this matter of food, because my mission is to make villages a thing of beauty. 7

We have to tackle the triple malady which holds our villages fast in its grip: (i) want of corporate sanitation; (ii) deficient diet; (iii) inertia. . . . They are not interested in their own welfare. They don't appreciate modern sanitary methods. They don't want to exert themselves beyond scratching their farms or doing such labour as they are used to. These difficulties are real and serious. But they must not baffle us. We must have an unquenchable faith in our mission. We must be patient with the people. We are ourselves novices in village work. We have to deal with a chronic disease. Patience and perseverance, if we have them, overcome mountains of difficulties. We are like nurses who may not leave their patients because they are reported to have an incurable disease. 8

The greatest education in the villages consists in the villagers being taught or induced to work methodically and profitably all the year round whether it be on the land or at industries connected with the villages. 9

I make bold to say that in spite of the crudeness which one sees among the villagers, class considered, in all that is good in human nature they compare favourably with any villagers in the world. This
testimony is borne out by the majority of travellers
who from the time of Huen Tsang down to the present
times have recorded their impressions. The innate
culture that the villages of India show, the art which
one sees in the homes of the poor, the restraint with
which the villagers conduct themselves, are surely
due to the religion that has bound them together
from time immemorial. 10

The Kisan or the peasant, whether as a landless labourer or a labouring proprietor, comes first.
He is the salt of the earth which rightly belongs or
should belong to him, not to the absentee landlord
or Zamindar. But in the non-violent way the labourer
cannot forcibly eject the absentee landlord. He has
so to work as to make it impossible for the landlord
to exploit him. Closest co-operation amongst the
peasants is absolutely necessary. To this end, special
organizing bodies or committees should be formed
where there are none and those already in existence
should be reformed where necessary. The Kisans
are for the most part illiterate. Both adults and
young persons of school-going age should be educated. This applies to men and women. Where they
are landless labourers their wages should be brought
to a level that would ensure a decent living which
should mean balanced food, dwelling houses and
clothing, which should satisfy health requirements. 11

If I have my say, our Governor-General and
our Premier would be drawn from the Kisans. In my

childhood I had learnt in the school books that the Kisans are heirs to the kingdom of the earth. This applies to those who labour on the land and eat from what they produce. Such Kisans to be worthy of high offices might be illiterate, provided they have robust common sense, great personal bravery, unimpeachable integrity and patriotism above suspicion. As real producers of wealth, they are verily the masters while we have enslaved them. It has been suggested to me that the higher secretariat posts should also be manned by Kisans. I would endorse this suggestion provided they are suitable and have knowledge of the work expected of them. When Kisans of this type are forthcoming I would publicly ask ministers and others to make room for them. *12*

CHAPTER 15

AGRICULTURE AND CATTLE WELFARE—II
LAND PROBLEM

Ownership of Land

The Kisan is the salt of the earth which rightly belongs or should belong to him, not to the absentee landlord or zamindar. *1*

Land and all property is his who will work it. Unfortunately the workers are or have been kept ignorant of this simple fact. *2*

I believe that the land you cultivate should belong to you, but it cannot be your own all at once, you cannot force it from the zamindars. Non-violence is the only way, consciousness of your own power is the only way. *3*

V.S.-7

No man should have more land than he needs for dignified sustenance. Who can dispute the fact that the grinding poverty of the masses is due to their having no land that they can call their own?

But it must be realized that the reform cannot be rushed. If it is to be brought about by non-violent means, it can only be done by education, both of the haves and the have-nots. The former should be assured that there never will be force used against them. The have-nots must be educated to know that no one can really compel them to do anything against their will, and that they can secure their freedom by learning the art of non-violence, i.e. self-suffering. *4*

Landlord and Tenant

I would tell you that ownership of your land belongs as much to the ryots as to you. *5*

I do not believe that the capitalists and the landlords are all exploiters by an inherent necessity, or that there is a basic or irreconcilable antagonism between their interests and those of the masses. . . . What is needed is not the extinction of landlords and capitalists, but a transformation of the existing relationship between them and the masses into something healthier and purer. *6*

My objective is to reach your heart and convert you so that you may hold all your private property in trust for your tenants and use it primarily for their welfare. I am aware of the fact that within the ranks of the Congress a new party, called the Socialist Party is coming into being, and I cannot say what would happen if that party succeeds in carrying the Congress with it. But I am quite clear that if

strictly honest and unchallengeable referendum of
our millions were to be taken, they would not vote
for the wholesale expropriation of the propertied
classes. I am working for the co-operation and co-
ordination of capital and labour, of landlord and
tenant. 7

But I must utter a note of warning. I have always told mill-owners that they are not exclusive
owners of mills and workmen are equal sharers in
ownership. In the same way, I would tell you that
ownership of your land belongs as much to the ryots
as to you, and you may not squander your gains in
luxurious or extravagant living, but must use them
for the well-being of ryots. Once you make your
ryots experience a sense of kinship with you and a
sense of security that their interests as members of a
family will never suffer at your hands, you may be
sure that there cannot be a clash between you and
them and no class war. 8

I do not want to destroy the zamindar, but
neither do I feel that the zamindar is inevitable. I
expect to convert the zamindars and other capitalists by the non-violent method, and therefore there
is for me nothing like an inevitability of class conflict. For it is an essential part of non-violence to go
along the line of least resistance. The moment the
cultivators of the soil realize their power, the zamindari evil will be sterilized. What can the poor zamindar do when they say that they will simply not work
the land unless they are paid enough to feed and
clothe and educate themselves and their children in
a decent manner. In reality the toiler is the owner of
what he produces. If the toilers intelligently combine,

they will become an irresistible power. That is
how I do not see the necessity of class conflict. If I
thought it inevitable, I should not hesitate to preach
it and teach it. 9

A model zamindar would at once reduce much
of the burden the ryot is now bearing. He would
come in intimate touch with the ryots and know
their wants and inject hope into them in the place of
despair which is killing the very life out of them.
He will not be satisfied with the ryots' ignorance
of the laws of sanitation and hygiene. He will reduce
himself to poverty in order that the ryot may have the
necessaries of life. He will study the economic condition of the ryots under his care, establish schools in
which he will educate his own children side by side
with those of the ryots. He will purify the village
well and the village tank. He will teach the ryot to
sweep his roads and clean his latrines by himself doing this necessary labour. He will throw open without reserve his own gardens for the unrestricted use
of the ryot. He will use as hospital, school, or the like
most of the unnecessary buildings which he keeps for
his pleasure. If only the capitalist class will read the
signs of the times, revise their notions of God-given
right to all they possess, in an incredibly short space
of time the seven hundred thousand dung-heaps
which today pass muster as villages can be turned
into abodes of peace, health and comfort. I am convinced that the capitalist, if he follows the Samurai
of Japan, has nothing really to lose and everything
to gain. There is no other choice than between
voluntary surrender on the part of the capitalist of
superfluities and consequent acquisition of the real
happiness of all on the one hand, and on the other,

the impending chaos into which, if the capitalist does not wake up betimes, awakened but ignorant, famishing millions will plunge the country and which not even the armed force that a powerful government can bring into play can avert. *10*

The zamindars would do well to take the time by the forelock. Let them cease to be mere rent collectors. They should become trustees and trusted friends of their tenants. They should limit their privy purse. Let them forgo the questionable perquisites they take from the tenants in the shape of forced gifts on marriage and other occasions, or *nazrana* on transfer of holdings from one Kisan to another or on restoration to the same Kisan after eviction for non-payment of rent. They should give them fixity of tenure, take a lively interest in their welfare, provide well-managed schools for their children, night-schools for adults, hospitals and dispensaries for the sick, look after the sanitation of villages and in a variety of ways make them feel that they, the zamindars, are their true friends taking only a fixed commission for their manifold services. In short they must justify their position. They should trust Congressmen. They may themselves become Congressmen and know that the Congress is a bridge between the people and the Government. All who have the true welfare of the people at heart can harness the services of the Congress. Congressmen will on their part see to it that Kisans scrupulously fulfil their obligations to the zamindars. I mean not necessarily the statutory, but the obligations which they have themselves admitted to be just. They must reject the doctrine that their holdings are absolutely theirs to the exclusion of the zamindars. They are or

should be members of a joint family in which the
zamindar is the head guarding their rights against
encroachment. Whatever the law may be, the
zamindari to be defensible must approach the conditions of a joint family.

I like the ideal of Rama and Janaka. They owned
nothing against the people. Everything including
themselves belonged to the people. They lived in
their midst a life not above theirs, but in correspondence with theirs. But these may not be regarded as
historical personages. Then let us take the example
of the great Caliph Omar. Though he was monarch
of a vast realm created by his great genius and amaz-
ing industry, he lived the life of a pauper and never
considered himself owner of the vast treasures that
lay at his feet. He was a terror to those officials who
squandered people's money in luxuries. *11*

To the landlords I say that if what is said against
them is true, I would warn them that their days
are numbered. They could no longer continue as
lords and masters. They have a bright future if they
become the trustees of the poor Kisans. He has in
mind not trustees in name but in reality. Such trustees
would take nothing for themselves that their labour
and care did not entitle them to. Then they would
find that no law would be able to touch them. The
Kisans would be their friends. *12*

It can be asked whether the present Rajas and
others can be expected to become trustees of the
poor. If they do not become trustees of their own
accord, force of circumstances will compel the
reform unless they court utter destruction. When

Panchayat Raj is established, public opinion will
do what violence can never do. The present power
of the zamindars, the capitalists and the Rajas can
hold sway only so long as the common people do
not realize their own strength. If the people non-co-
operate with the evil of zamindari or capitalism,
it must die of inanition. In Panchayat Raj only the
Panchayat will be obeyed and the Panchayat can only
work through the laws of their making. *13*

Real socialism has been handed down to us by
our ancestors who taught: 'All land belongs to
Gopal, where then is the boundary line? Man is the
maker of that line and he can therefore unmake
it.' Gopal literally means shepherd; it also means
God. In modern language it means the State, i. e.
the People. That the land today does not belong to
the people is too true. But the fault is not in the
teaching. It is in us who have not lived up to it.

I have no doubt that we can make as good an
approach to it as is possible for any nation, not excluding Russia, and that without violence. The most
effective substitute for violent dispossession is the
wheel with all its implications. Land and all property
is his who will work it. Unfortunately the workers are
or have been kept ignorant of this simple fact. *14*

In the non-violent order of the future, the land
would belong to the State, for had it not been said
'*sabhi bhumi Gopalki*'? Under such dispensation, there
would be no waste of talents and labour. This would
be impossible through violent means. It was therefore
a truism to say that the utter ruin of the landowner
brought about through violence would also involve
the ruin of the labourers in the end. If the land-
owners, therefore, acted wisely, no party would lose. *15*

CHAPTER 16

AGRICULTURE AND CATTLE WELFARE—III

CO-OPERATION

The most important question for consideration
. . . was whether cow farming should be in the
hands of individuals or done collectively. I myself
had no hesitation in saying that she could never be
saved by individual farming. Her salvation, and with
her that of buffalo, could only be brought about
by collective endeavour. It is quite impossible for an
individual farmer to look after the welfare of his
cattle in his own home in a proper and scientific manner. Amongst other causes lack of collective effort
has been a principal cause of the deterioration of
the cow and hence of cattle in general.

The world today is moving towards the ideal of
collective or co-operative effort in every department
of life. Much in this line has been and is being accomplished. It has come into our country also, but
in such a distorted form that our poor have not been
able to reap its benefits. *Pari Passu* with the increase
in our population land holdings of the average farmer
are daily decreasing. Moreover what the individual
possesses is often fragmentary. For such farmers to
keep cattle in their homes is a suicidal policy; and
yet this is their condition today. Those who give the
first place to economics and pay scant attention to
religious, ethical or humanitarian considerations
proclaim from the housetops that the farmer is being
devoured by his cattle due to the cost of their feed

which is out of all proportion to what they yield.
They say it is folly not to slaughter wholesale all useless animals.

What then should be done by humanitarians
is the question. The answer obviously is to find a way
whereby we may not only save the lives of our cattle
but also see that they do not become a burden. I am
sure that co-operative effort can help us in a large
measure.

The following comparison may be helpful:

1.   Under the collective system no farmer can
keep cattle in his house as he does today. They foul
the air, and dirty the surroundings. There is neither intelligence nor humanitarianism in living with
animals. Man was not meant to do so. The space
taken up by the cattle today would be spared to the
farmer and his family, if the collective system were
adopted.

2.   As the number of cattle increases, life becomes
impossible for the farmer in his home. Hence he is
obliged to sell the calves and kill the male buffaloes
or else turn them out to starve and die. This inhumanity would be averted, if the care of cattle
were undertaken on a co-operative basis.

3.   Collective cattle farming would ensure the
supply of veterinary treatment to animals when they
are ill. No ordinary farmer can afford this on his
own.

4.   Similarly one selected bull can be easily kept
for the need of several cows under the collective
system. This is impossible otherwise except for
charity.

5. Common grazing ground or land for exercising the animals will be easily available under the co-operative system, whereas today generally there is nothing of the kind for individual farmers.

6. The expense on fodder will be comparatively far less under the collective system.

7. The sale of milk at good prices will be greatly facilitated, and there will be no need or temptation for the farmer to adulterate it as he does as an individual.

8. It is impossible to carry out tests of the fitness of every head of cattle individually, but this could easily be done for the cattle of a whole village and would thus make it easier to improve the breed.

9. The foregoing advantages should be sufficient argument in favour of co-operative farming. The strongest argument in its favour is that the individualistic system has been the means of making our own conditions as well as that of our cattle pitiable. We can only save ourselves and them by making this essential change.

I firmly believe too that we shall not derive the full benefits of agriculture until we take to co-operative farming. Does it not stand to reason that it is far better for a hundred families in a village to cultivate their lands collectively and divide the income therefrom than to divide the land anyhow into a hundred portions? And what applied to land applies equally to cattle.

It is quite another matter that it may be difficult to convert people to adopt this way of life straight-away. The straight and narrow road is always hard to traverse. Every step in the programme of cow service is strewn with thorny problems. But only by surmounting difficulties can we hope to make the path easier. My purpose for the time being is to show the great superiority of collective cattle farming over the individual effort. I hold further that the latter is wrong and the former only is right. In reality even the individual can only safeguard his independence through co-operation. In cattle farming the individual effort has led to selfishness and inhumanity, whereas the collective effort can abate both the evils, if it does not remove them altogether. *1*

'Should peasants pool together their land and divide the crop in proportion to the area of the fields they hold?'

My notion of co-operation is that the land would be held in co-operation by the owners and tilled and cultivated also in co-operation. This would cause a saving of labour, capital, tools, etc. The owners would work in co-operation and own capital, tools, animals, seeds etc. in co-operation. Co-operative farming of my conception would change the face of the land and banish poverty and idleness from their midst. All this is only possible if people become friends of one another and as one family. When that happy event takes place there would be no ugly sore in the form of a communal problem. *2*

The system of co-operation is far more necessary for the agriculturists. The land belongs to the State; therefore, it yields the largest return when it is worked co-operatively.

Let it be remembered that co-operation should be based on strict non-violence. There is no such thing as success of violent co-operation. Hitler was a forcible example of the latter. He also talked vainly of co-operation which was forced upon the people and everyone knew where Germany had been led as a result.

It would be a sad thing if India also tries to build up the new society based on co-operation by means of violence. Good brought about through force destroyed individuality. Only when the change is effected through the persuasive power of non-violent non-co-operation, i.e. love, could the foundation of individuality be preserved, and real, abiding progress be assured for the world. 3

CHAPTER 17

AGRICULTURE AND CATTLE WELFARE—IV

MANURE

Compost Manure

An All India Compost Conference was held in New Delhi during the month (of December 1947) to consider the question of compost development on the widest scale possible. It was the conception of Shrimati Mirabehn and was presided over by Dr. Rajendraprasad. Sardar Datar Singh, Dr. Acharya and other eminent men in the line took part in it. Several important resolutions were passed by it on schemes for towns and villages. A sub-committee consisting of Shrimati Mirabehn, Shri Shivakumar Sharma, Dr. B. N. Lal and Dr. K. G. Joshi (with Dr. B. N. Lal as convener) was appointed to prepare a skeleton scheme for the

provinces. The resolutions emphasized the necessity of "the agricultural utilization of town sewage,
sullage and sludge, the utilization of the by-products
of the slaughter house and other trade wastes (for
example, wool waste, mill waste, leather waste, etc.)
and for the composting of other materials like
water-hyacinth, cane-trash, press-mud, forest
leaves etc."

These resolutions are good and useful if they do
not remain merely on paper. The chief thing is whether they would be reduced to practice throughout
India. To do so would tax the resources of many
Mirabehns. Given the willing co-operation of the masses of India, this country can not only drive
out the shortage of food, but can provide India with
more than enough. This organic manure ever en-
riches, never impoverishes the soil. The daily waste,
judiciously composted, returns to the soil in the
form of golden manure causing a saving of millions
of rupees and increasing manifold, the total yield of
grains and pulses. In addition, the judicious use of
waste keeps the surroundings clean. And cleanliness
is not only next to godliness, it promotes health. [1]

One potent way of increasing production is
proper manuring. Artificial manures, I am told,
are harmful to the soil. The compost manure emit
no bad odour. It would save lakhs of rupees and
also increase the fertility of the soil without exhaus-
ting it. [2]

Manure Pits

[Generally agreeing with Mr. Brayne's suggestions regarding
the need for pulverizing manure pits in villages, but at the same
time differing from him in his view that the pits should be six
feet wide and six feet deep, Gandhiji wrote as under:]

I know that the pits such as Mr. Brayne suggests are generally recommended. In my opinion,
however, superficial burial recommended by Poore
is more scientific and more remunerative. The cost
of digging is lessened and that of removal avoided
altogether or certainly lessened. Add to this the fact
that the excreta are turned into manure in almost
a week's time, for the reason that the bacteria,
which live within six or nine inches of the surface of
the earth, and the air and the rays of the sun, act
upon the excreta and turn them into sweet manure
much more quickly than when the refuse is buried
deep.

But the chief thing to remember is not the
various methods of disposing of refuse, so much as
the necessity of burying all the refuse for the double
purpose of promoting the villagers' health and their
material condition, through the better yield of their
crops which the manure must produce. It should
be remembered that organic rubbish other than
excreta must be separately buried. 3

Night-soil as Manure

G. I. Fowler states, in his *Wealth and Waste* that
a proper disposal of human excreta would realize
Rs. 2 per head per year. In the vast majority of cases,
all this rich manure is being wasted and disease
invited. He quotes Prof. Brultini, from his volume
The Use of Waste Materials, who says that "nitrogen
derived from the 282,000 residents of Delhi is sufficient to fertilize a minimum of 10,000 and a maximum of 95,000 acres." Because we do not know how
to treat our scavengers, Delhi of ancient fame has
pestilential spots of which we have to feel ashamed.

If we all become scavengers, we would know how to treat ourselves and how to turn what today is poison into rich food for plant life. 30 crores of the population of India should mean, according to Dr. Fowler, an annual gain of 60 crores of rupees to the country, if we would but make a wise use of human excreta. *4*

Preparation of Compost Manure

[There is in Indore an Institute of Plant Industry. It issues from time to time leaflets for those whom it is designed to serve. The first one of these describes the utility and the method of preparing compost manure from farm wastes. As it is valuable for Harijans and village workers who handle cattle-dung and night-soil, I copy below practically the whole of the leaflet incorporating footnotes into the running description of the process.

—M. K. G.]

It has long been recognized that adequate and systematic recuperation of organic matter in Indian soils must be part of any successful scheme for intensive agriculture. It is also equally understood that the available sources of farm yard manure cannot supply the quantities needed, apart from the fact that during the making a large portion of the nitrogen is lost and the final product takes a very long time to attain the most efficient physical condition. Green manuring is perhaps a possible substitute, but under monsoon conditions it is uncertain in most parts of India. The decomposition of green manure in the soil also interferes for the time being with the natural processes of recuperation of available plant food in the soil which 'lay a very substantial part in the maintenance of soil fertility in tropical regions. It is clearly the best course to relieve the soil of the burden of manufacturing humus and enable it to concentrate solely upon the work of recuperation and crop growth. The simplest way of doing this is to prepare humus as a by-product during the routine of farm work, utilizing all agricultural wastes which are not needed as fuel or fodder.

It should be emphasized at this stage that any substitute for farm yard manure must closely resemble humus in composition, and the Indore method aims at and achieves this. The object of the Indore method thus differs radically from that of processes where the aim is to produce a highly nitrogenous active manure whose special utility is similar to that of artificials.

The work carried out at the Institute of Plant Industry at Indore, which was the final outcome of twenty years' attempts by Mr. Albert Howard in this direction, has now proved definitely that these principles can very easily be put into actual practice. The Indore method of compost making supplies a practical technique and opens new avenues for development. The unlimited resources of natural wastes both from the farm and the towns can thus be tapped for use in agriculture. A copious supply of manure is made possible without having recourse to any unnatural measures such as encroaching upon the use of dung as fuel and the export of oil-cakes, at the same time securing economy in the use of artificials which give their best results when reinforced with organic matter.

The problems and underlying principles involved have been discussed and the elaboration of the Indore method described in the *Utilization of Agricultural Waste* (Howard and Wad, Oxford University Press, 1931). This article gives only a brief working outline of the process as applicable to the Indian cultivator's conditions.

The value of farm yard manure is appreciated in the case of irrigated crops in India, but periodic moderate dressings to fields under dry cultivation are equally essential. The Indore compost method quickly produces larger amounts of richer manure, which is moreover, actively useful to crops immediately on application, which is not always the case with farm yard manure. Indore compost is ready for use after three months, when properly prepared, and is then a dark-brown or coffee-coloured amorphous substance, containing about 20 per cent of partially decomposed coarse material readily crushed between the fingers, the rest being fine enough when wet (and the colloidal particles therefore swollen) to pass through a sieve of 6 meshes per linear inch. The nitrogen content varies from .8 per cent to 1.0 per cent or more according to the nature of the wastes used. About fifty cartloads of compost per pair of bullocks can easily be made each year by the use of only one-fourth of the fresh dung along with 100 to 125 cartloads of farm wastes of all kinds and half of the quantity of urine-soaked earth which is available from the cattle-shed. The remaining half is also a good manure and can be added directly to fields. If more residues are available, all the dung and urine earth can be utilized to make about 150 cartloads of compost. The cost of making is 8½ annas per cartload of ripe compost at Indore rates of wages (men 7 annas, women 5 annas per day of eight hours).

Outline of Indore Method

The main feature of the process is to decompose

rapidly a mixture of otherwise useless farm wastes with fresh dung, wood ash and urine earth in pits. The pits should not be deeper than 2 feet and should be 14 feet in breadth. A convenient length is 30 feet. This suits both large and small scale work; for instance a portion 3 feet in length can be filled in 6 days with bedding from under 2 pairs of bullocks. The adjacent portion is next filled, each being subsequently treated as a separate unit. The material is uniformly moistened with a slurry of water containing small quantities of dung, wood ash, urine earth, and fungus starter from an active pit. Actively decomposing compost soon becomes white with fungus growth. This material is then used to start vigorous decomposition in a fresh charge. For the first time when no starter is available fungus growth is stimulated by the addition of a small quantity of green leaves to the bedding when made. Full activity is attained in the starter after 3 to 4 generations. The activity is then kept up by regulating moisture and air by means of surface waterings and turnings assisted by a second addition of starter, this time taken from a pit more than 30 days old. The mass soon becomes very hot and remains so for a long time. The systematic handling secures a good mixture (as shown by its uniform appearance) and a copious air supply at every stage. Moderate watering begins decomposition at once, which continues without a break to the end, producing a very uniform final product.

The Making of Pits

Select a well-drained area near the cattle-shed and if possible near a source of water supply. Dig out one foot of earth and spread it on all sides to make a pit, 30 feet by 14 feet by 2 feet; such pits should be arranged in pairs, the long side being east to west. The distance between two pits in a pair should be six feet and the pairs themselves should be twelve feet apart. The final heaps and monsoon heaps are made on these broad spaces which are also useful for removal of manure by carts directly from each heap.

Earth and Urine

The urine passed by cattle is rich in valuable manurial matter and this is mostly wasted in the usual method of making farm yard manure. A pakka-floor in the cattle-shed is both costly and unsuitable for the bullocks. A soft, warm and dry bed on which cattle may rest and sleep can be made cheaply of loose earth. Convenient sources are threshing-floor sweepings, silt from choked drains and earth from silage pits. A flat 6 inches layer is sufficient to absorb all urine without nuisance, if wet patches are scrapped daily and thinly covered by a little fresh earth and with uneaten fodder from the manger over it. This urine earth should be removed and replaced every four months by a fresh layer. The finer portion should be reserved for compost making and the bigger lumps directly added to fields. It is a rapidly acting manure specially suitable as a top-dressing for any irrigated crop.[5]

Cow-dung and Ash

Only a quarter of the daily supply of fresh dung is needed; this is applied as liquid 'slurry', being mixed with water; the rest can be made into fuel if required. Wood ashes from the kitchen and other places should be carefully collected and stored under cover.

Farm Wastes or Kuchra

Every type of vegetable waste not otherwise needed on the farm can be made into compost, e.g. weeds, stalks of cotton, pigeon pea, sesamum, safflower, niger, linseed, rape, black and green gram, sugarcane trash, stools of juar, and sugarcane, fallen leaves of trees and uneaten residues of grass, straw, juar and other fodders. Hard materials require cracking. This has been successfully done, even on soft unmetalled roads in Sind, by simply spreading such material on a cart track and periodically removing crushed portions and replacing them by unbroken stuff. Very hard residues like stumps and roots require (in addition to cracking) soaking in water for at least two days, or burial with moist earth for two to three months before they can be successfully utilized. The latter can be done easily during the monsoon period. Green materials must be partially dried and then stacked. Small amounts of various kinds of residues should be stacked together, while separate ganjis, i.e. stacks, must be made for larger quantities of any single material. At the time of removing to the compost pit care must be taken to get a mixture of all types, no single material ever exceeding ⅛ of the total amount thus removed. The very hard soaked or softened residues should be used only in very small quantities at a time. This is really automatically achieved by the proportions of different residues normally available if they are stored and used in quantities which will ensure a steady supply all round the year. The quality of the compost can be further improved by using for it a kharif-sown

catch-crop of *sann* or other legume harvested green,
and stacked after withering. The land will be clear
in time to sow a *rabi* crop which will also benefit
by the *sann* having been grown.

Water

It is a saving of labour and an advantage if
household waste water is led to a small pit or sunk
tub near the compost area and utilized every day.
Any kind of water which has long been lying stag-
nant is harmful. Additional water required must be
secured by other means. Between 50 to 60 four-gallon
kerosene tins of water are necessary to prepare one
cartload of compost according to season.

The Process in Detail

Filling the pits with bedding: Take a *pal* or a
stretcher made of a piece of gunny sacking 4 feet by
3 feet, the longer edges being fastened to two bamboos
each 7 feet 6 inches long. Up to one *palful* of farm
wastes for each bullock and one and a half *pals* for
each buffalo should be spread every day on the
floor of the cattle-shed on which the cattle rest and
sleep. The material thus gets impregnated with
urine as well as mixed and crushed by the animals.
The bedding in the rainy season is made by sand-
witching a layer of green withered stuff between two
of dry wastes specially reserved for the purpose. Fresh
dung left over after making the slurry can either
be made into *kurdas*, i.e. dried dung cakes, or spread
over the bedding in lumps not bigger than a small
orange. The portion of the urine earth and fungus
starter also left over after making the slurry is then
scattered over the bedding next morning when it is

removed by spades and *pals* from end to end of the
floor to be directly dropped in pits and spread in thin
layers by rakes. Every such layer is then moistened
uniformly by the slurry containing ash, dung, earth
and fungus starter in small amounts. After the removal of all bedding the floor is swept of all finer portions which are then added to the pit as a surface
layer. The top layer is wetted by sprinkled water and
soaking is completed by further sprinklings in the
evening and next morning. A pit, or a portion of it
according to the quantity of waste material available, must be filled to the top in six days. A fresh
charge in another portion or pit should then be
begun. Trampling while charging is *harmful* as air is
excluded.

During the monsoon rains the pits get full of
water. When the rains begin the contents should be
removed and heaped on ground level taking advantage of the routine turnings. During the rains fresh
compost should be made on the ground in heaps
8 feet by 8 feet by 2 feet with vertical sides, and closely
grouped together on the broad spaces so that they are
protected from cold winds.

Turning and Watering of Compost

The surface of the decomposing compost is kept
moist by weekly sprinkling of water. It is necessary to restore moisture and air in the interior at
intervals and hence 3 turns have to be given, accompanied by watering to make up for lost moisture.
In wet weather the quantity of these waterings may
be lessened or no water may be added, but the water
during the first filling or stacking must be added in
all seasons.

First Turn after about 15 Days

Remove the undecomposed surface layer from the whole pit and use it as part filling for a fresh pit. Scatter compost about 30 days old over the exposed surface and sprinkle water over the top till well moistened for about six inches. During this first turning the pit is divided lengthwise and the half on the windward side is left undisturbed. The other half is then thrown over it (a wooden rake is convenient for this). The material should not be taken off layer after layer but as far as possible from the top to the bottom of the pit by a vertical or slanting stroke. Every layer of the turned material, about six inches thick, must be soaked with sprinkled water. In the monsoon the whole heap may be turned to avoid too much height.

Second Turn after One Month

The material in one half of the pit is simply raked as above on to the other vacant side of the pit with adequate watering, the same care to mix it from top to bottom being taken.

Third Turn at the End of Two Months

The compost is similarly transferred by shovels to the surface on the broad spaces and watered. The material from two pits can be conveniently shovelled on to the space between to make one heap 10 feet broad and $3\frac{1}{2}$ feet high; the length is immaterial and several pits or heaps can thus be stored together. If convenient the manure after moistening well may be directly carted from pits to the field. The heap should be made on the spot where the product is to be used, thus saving valuable time at the sowing season. All heaps should be dressed to vertical sides and flat tops to prevent excessive drying which stops decomposition.

Good compost gives no smell at any stage and the appearance is uniform throughout. If smell or flies appear it is a sign that more air is wanted and the pit should therefore be turned and a little ash and dung added.

The quantities required in individual cases can easily be found out by simple calculations with the help of the following data:

Quantities Required for 40 Animals

Filling into pits every day for six days:

Bedding and sweepings removed to the pit in one day; 40 to 50 *pals* after scattering on it 4 *tagaris*, i.e. sheet iron basins being 18 inches diameter by 6 inches depth, of fungus starter, 15 of urine earth and excess of dung if not used as fuel.

Slurry: For one day's output from cattle-shed 20 kerosene tins (4 gallons) of water, 5 *tagaris* of dung, 1 *tagari* of ash, 1 *tagari* of urine earth, and 2 *tagaris* of fungus starter.

Water: For one day's output from cattle-shed 6 tins immediately after filling, 10 tins in the evening and 6 next morning.

Surface waterings: 25 tins each time.

Water at turning time: 1st turn 60 to 100 tins, 2nd turn 40 to 60 tins, 3rd turn 40 to 80 tins according to season.

Fungus starter at the time of 1st turn: *12 tagaris.*

TABLE

Volume (in double handfuls) and weights (in lb.) of the contents of a *tagari* or basket.

Material	Volume in double-handfuls	Weight in lb.
Fresh dung	6 to 7	40
Urine earth	20 to 21	22
Wood ashes	15	20
Fungus starter	5	20
For 1st turn starter	6	20

TIME TABLE OF OPERATIONS

Days	Events
1	Filling begins
6	Filling ends
10	Fungus established
12	First watering
15 } 16 }	First turn and addition of one month old compost
24	Second watering
30 } 32 }	Second turn
38	Third watering
45	Fourth watering
60	Third turn
67	Fifth watering
75	Sixth watering
90	Compost ready for use

When circumstances do not permit the adoption of the Indore process in full detail its advantages may be partially secured in the following way:

The mixed waste is used as bedding for cattle and the requisite amounts of dung, urine earth and ash scattered over it next morning before removal as already described. The material is then carried to the margin of a field where the manure is to be used, or to some other suitable well-drained place, and stored in heaps not more than 3 inches high and 8 inches broad, and of any convenient length. After the rains have set in the fungus will establish itself in about a month. One full turn is then given choosing a cloudy or moderately rainy day. Another turn or two after an interval of a month will cause the material to rot by the end of the season, given a favourable distribution of rainfall.

A year of waiting is, of course, necessary before the manure is ready and possibly longer if the rains fails seriously.

The resulting manure, though probably rather inferior to compost made in the standard way, will be undoubtedly better than ordinary farm yard manure, for even by this modified process hard, woody waste can be rotted easily, thus giving a far larger quantity of manure than is produced in existing village practice. 6

Village Crops

Every village's first concern will be to grow its own food crops and cotton for its cloth. It should have a reserve for its cattle, recreation and playground for adults and children. Then if there is more land available, it will grow *useful* money crops, thus excluding *ganja*, tobacco, opium and the like. 7

CHAPTER 18

AGRICULTURE AND CATTLE WELFARE—V

THE PROBLEM OF SCARCITY OF FOOD

Food Shortage

India is not unfamiliar with starvation and death of tens of thousands, if not millions, due to famine, natural or man-made. I claim that in a well-ordered society there should be always pre-arranged methods of successful treatment of scarcity of water and food crops. This is, however, not the occasion for describing a well-ordered society and for showing how it would deal with the matter. Our concern, for the present, is to see whether we can, with fair hope of success, deal with the present food crisis.

I think we can. The first lesson we must learn is of self-help and self-reliance. If we assimilate this lesson, we shall at once free ourselves from disastrous dependence upon foreign countries and ultimate bankruptcy. This is not said in arrogance but as a matter of fact. We are not a small place, dependent for its food supply upon outside help. We are a sub-continent, a nation of nearly 400 millions. We are a country of mighty rivers and a rich variety of agricultural land, with inexhaustible cattle-wealth. That our cattle give much less milk than we need is entirely our own fault. Our cattle-wealth is any day capable of giving us all milk we need. Our country, if it had not been neglected during the past few centuries, should today not only be providing herself with sufficient food, but also be playing a useful role in supplying the outside world with much-needed foodstuffs of which the late war has unfortunately left practically the whole world in want. This does not exclude India. The distress is growing instead of showing signs of decreasing. My suggestion does not include ungrateful rejection of free supply that any foreign country may wish to offer us. All I say is that we must not go a-begging. It demoralizes. Add to this the difficulty of internal transport of foodstuffs from one place to another. We have not the requisite facility for rapid movement of grains and other foodstuffs from place to place. Further add not the remote possibility of delivery of uneatable stuff. We dare not lose sight of the fact that we have to deal with human nature. In no part of the world it is to be found perfect or even very nearly so.

Next, let us see what possible foreign aid we can get. I am told, not more than three per cent of our present wants. If this information is correct and I have had it checked by several experts who confirm the figure, I am sure the case for reliance on outside help falls to the ground. The slightest dependence on outside help is likely to deflect us from trying to the fullest extent our immense internal possibilities in the shape of utilizing every inch of arable land for growing crops for daily food in the place of growing money crops. We must reclaim waste land which is capable of being placed under immediate cultivation.

Centralization of foodstuffs, I apprehend, is ruinous. Decentralization easily deals a blow to black-marketing, saves time and money in transport to and fro. Moreover, the villager who grows India's cereals and pulses knows how to save his crops against rodents. The movement of grain from station to station makes it liable to be eaten by rodents. This costs the country many millions and deprives it of tons of grain, every ounce of which we badly need. If every Indian were to realize the necessity of growing food wherever it can be grown, we should most probably forget that there was scarcity of foodstuffs in the land. I have by no means dealt fully with the fascinating and absorbing subject of growing more food, but I hope I have said enough to stimulate interest and turn the wise towards the thought of how every individual can help in the laudable enterprise.

Let me now show how to deal with the three per cent of grains we might possibly get from outside. Hindus observe a fast or a semi-fast every eleventh day per fortnight. Muslims and others are not prohibited from denying themselves especially when it is for the sake of the starving millions. If the whole nation realized the beauty of this partial self-denial, India would more than cover the deficit caused by the voluntary deprivation of foreign aid.

Personally I hold that rationing has very limited use if any. If the producers were left to themselves, they would bring their produce to the market and everyone would get good and eatable grain, which today is not easily obtainable.

I shall close this hurried review of the food crisis by drawing attention to President Truman's reported advice to the American people that they should eat less bread, and thus save the much-needed grain for starving Europe. He added that Americans would not lose in health by the recommended act of self-denial. I tender my congratulations to President Truman on this philanthropic gesture. I must decline to endorse the suggestion that at the back of this philanthropy there is the sordid motive of deriving a pecuniary advantage for America. A man must be judged by his action, not the motive prompting it. God alone knows men's hearts. If America would deny herself for the sake of hungry Europe, should we fail to do this little act of self-denial for ourselves? If many must die of starvation let us at least earn the credit of having done our best in the way of self-help which ennobles a nation. *1*

In Times of Scarcity

He who saves gains as much, that is to say, he produces as much. Hence those who feel for the poor, those who would be one with them must curtail their wants. There are many ways. I shall only mention some here. There is much, too much food eaten and wasted by the well-to-do.

Use one grain at a time. *Chapati*, rice and pulses, milk, ghee, *gur*, and oil are used in ordinary households besides vegetables and fruit. I regard this as an unhealthy combination. Those who get animal protein in the shape of milk, cheese, eggs or meat need not use pulses at all. The poor people get only vegetable protein. If the well-to-do give up pulses and oils, they set free these two essentials for the poor who get neither animal protein nor animal fat. Then the grain eaten should not be sloppy. Half the quantity suffices when it is eaten dry and not dipped in any gravy. It is well to eat it with raw salads such as onion, carrot, radish, salad leaves, tomatoes. An ounce or two of salads serves the purpose of eight ounces of cooked vegetables. *Chapatis* or bread should not be eaten with milk. To begin with, one meal may be raw vegetables and *chapati* or bread, and the other cooked vegetables with milk or curds.

Sweet dishes should be eliminated altogether. Instead *gur* or sugar in small quantities may be taken with milk or bread or by itself.

Fresh fruit is good to eat, but only a little is necessary to give one to the system. It is an expensive article, and an over-indulgence by the well-to-do has deprived the poor and the ailing of an article which they need much more than the well-to-do.

Any medical man who has studied the science of dietetics will certify that what I have suggested can do no harm to the body, on the contrary it must conduce to better health.

This is only one way of saving foodstuff. It is obvious. But by itself it cannot produce much visible effect.

Grain-dealers have to shed their greed and the habit of making as much profit as possible. They must be satisfied with as little as possible. They run the risk of being looted, if they do not gain the credit of being keepers of grain for the sake of the poor. They should be in touch with the people in their neighbourhood.

By far the most important part of the work consists in educating the villagers to keep what they have and to induce cultivation of fresh crops wherever water is available. This requires widespread and intelligent propaganda. It is not generally known that bananas, potatoes, beetroot, yam and *suran*, and in a measure pumpkin are a food crop easily grown. They can take the place of bread in time of need.

There is too scarcity of money. There may be grain available but no money to buy it with. There is no money because there is no employment. This has to be found. Spinning is the readiest and the handiest. But local needs may supply other sources of labour. Every available source has to be tapped so that there is no want of employment. Only the lazy ones need and must starve. Patient handling will induce even this class to shed their laziness. 2

In the circumstances (of food crisis) the following things should be attended to at once:

1. Every person should confine his daily wants regarding food to the minimum, consistent with his or her health requirements; and where, as in cities, milk, vegetables, oil and fruit are available, grains and pulses should be reduced as they easily can be. Starch can be derived from starchy roots such as carrots, parsnips, potatoes, yam, bananas; the idea being to exclude from present diet and conserve those grains and pulses which can be kept and stored. Vegetables too should not be eaten as an indulgence or for pleasure, when millions are denied the use of these things altogether and are now threatened with starvation due to shortage of cereals and pulses.

2. Everyone who has access to any water should try himself or herself to grow some edible for personal or general use. The easiest way to do so is to collect clean earth, mix it with organic manure where possible—even a little bit of dried cowdung is good organic manure—and put it in any earthen or tin pot and throw some seeds of vegetables such as mustard and cress etc. and daily water the pots. They will be surprised how quickly the seeds sprout

and give edible leaves which need not even be cooked but can be eaten in the form of salad.

3. All flower gardens should be utilized for growing edibles. And in this connection I would suggest to the Viceroy, Governors and high officials to take the lead. I would ask the heads of agricultural departments at the Centre and Provinces to flood the country with leaflets in the provincial languages telling laymen how and what to grow easily.

4. Reduction should be taken up not merely by the civilian population but equally, if not predominantly, by the military. I say predominantly, for the military ranks being under rigid military discipline can easily carry out measures of economy.

5. All exports of seeds, such as oil seeds, oils, oil cakes, nuts, etc., should be stopped, if they have not been already. Oil cakes, if the seeds are sifted of earth and foreign matter, are good human food with rich protein content.

6. Deep wells should be sunk by the Government wherever possible and required, whether for irrigation or for drinking purposes.

7. Given hearty co-operation by Government servants and the general public, I have not the slightest doubt that the country can tide over the difficulty. Just as panic is the surest way to defeat, so also will be the case when there is widespread distress impending and prompt action is not taken. Let us not think of the cause of the distress. Whatever the cause, the fact is that if the Government and the public do not approach the crisis patiently and courageously, disaster is a certainty.

8. Above all, black-marketing and dishonesty should disappear altogether and willing co-operation

between all parties should be the order of the day in so far as this crisis is concerned. 3

Food Shortage and Over-population

If it is contended that birth-control is necessary for the nation because of over-population, I dispute the proposition. It has never been proved. In my opinion, by a proper land-system, better agriculture and a supplementary industry, this country is capable of supporting twice as many people as there are today.

This little globe of ours is not a toy of yesterday. It has not suffered from the weight of over-population through its age of countless millions. How can it be that it is in danger of perishing of shortage of food unless birth rate is checked through the use of contraceptives? 4

CHAPTER 19

KHADI AND SPINNING

Khadi connotes the beginning of economic freedom and equality of all in the country. It must be taken with all its implications. It means a wholesale Swadeshi mentality, a determination to find all the necessaries of life in India and that too through the labour and intellect of the villagers. The latter will be largely self-contained and will voluntarily serve the cities of India and even the outside world in so far as it benefits both the parties.

This needs a revolutionary change in the mentality and tastes of many. Easy though the non-violent way is in many respects, it is very difficult in many others. It vitally touches the life of every single Indian, makes him feel aglow with the possession of a power that has lain hidden within himself, and makes him proud of his identity with every drop of the ocean of Indian humanity.

Khadi to me is the symbol of unity of Indian humanity, of its economic freedom and equality and, therefore, ultimately in the poetic expression of Jawaharlal Nehru, 'the livery of India's freedom'.

Moreover, Khadi mentality means decentralization of the production and distribution of the necessaries of life. Therefore, the formula so far evolved is, every village to produce all its necessaries and a certain percentage in addition for the requirements of the cities.

Having explained the implications of Khadi, I must indicate what Congressmen can and should do towards its promotion. Production of Khadi includes cotton growing, picking, ginning, cleaning, carding, slivering, spinning, sizing, dyeing, preparing the warp and the woof, weaving, and washing. These, with the exception of dyeing, are essential processes. Every one of them can be effectively handled in the villages and is being so handled in many villages throughout India which the A. I. S. A. is covering.

If Congressmen will be true to their Congress call in respect of Khadi, they will carry out the instructions of the A. I. S. A. issued from time to time as to the part they can play in Khadi planning. Only a few broad rules can be laid down here:

1. Every family with a plot of ground can grow cotton at least for family use. Cotton growing is an easy process. In Bihar the cultivators were by law

compelled to grow indigo on $\frac{3}{20}$ of their cultivable land. This was in the interest of the foreign indigo planter. Why cannot we grow cotton voluntarily for the nation on a certain portion of our land? The reader will note that decentralization commences from the beginning of the Khadi processes. Today cotton crop is centralized and has to be sent to distant parts of India. Before the war it used to be sent principally to Britain and Japan. It was and still is a money crop and, therefore, subject to the fluctuations of the market. Under the Khadi scheme cotton growing becomes free from this uncertainty and gamble. The grower grows what he needs. The farmer needs to know that his first business is to grow for his own needs. When he does that, he will reduce the chance of a low market ruining him.

2. Every spinner would buy—if he has not his own—enough cotton for ginning, which he can easily do without the hand-ginning roller frame. He can gin his own portion with a board and an iron rolling pin. Where this is considered impracticable, hand-ginned cotton should be bought and carded. Carding for self can be done well on a tiny bow without much effort. The greater the decentralization of labour, the simpler and cheaper the tools. The slivers made, the process of spinning commences.

Imagine the unifying and educative effect of the whole nation simultaneously taking part in the processes up to spinning! Consider the levelling effect of the bond of common labour between the rich and the poor!

If Congressmen will put their heart into the work, they will make improvements in the tools and make many discoveries. In our country there has been a divorce between labour and intelligence. The result has been stagnation. If there is an indissoluble marriage between the two, and that in the manner here suggested, the resultant good will be inestimable.

In this scheme of nation-wide spinning as a sacrifice, I do not expect the average man or woman to give more than one hour daily to this work. *1*

The message of the spinning wheel is much wider than its circumference. Its message is one of simplicity, service of mankind, living so as not to hurt others, creating an indissoluble bond between the rich and the poor, capital and labour, the prince and the peasant. *2*

I stand by what is implied in the phrase, 'unto this last'. We must do even unto this last as we would have the world do by us. All must have equal opportunity. Given the opportunity, every human being has the same possibility for spiritual growth. That is what the spinning wheel symbolizes. *3*

I can only think of spinning as the fittest and most acceptable sacrificial body labour. I cannot imagine anything nobler or more national than that for, say one hour in the day, we should all do the labour that the poor must do, and thus identify ourselves with them and through them with all mankind. I cannot imagine better worship of God than that in His name I should labour for the poor even as they do. The spinning wheel spells a more equitable distribution of the riches of the earth. *4*

I feel convinced that the revival of hand-spinning and hand-weaving will make the largest contribution to the economic and the moral regeneration of India. The millions must have a simple industry to supplement agriculture. Spinning was the cottage industry years ago, and if the millions are to be saved from starvation, they must be enabled to reintroduce spinning in their homes and every village must re-possess its own weaver. 5

If the reader would visualize the picture of the Indian skeleton, he must think of the eighty per cent of the population which is working its own fields, and which has practically no occupation for at least four months in the year, and which therefore lives on the borderland of starvation. This is the normal condition. The ever recurring famines make a large addition to this enforced idleness. What is the work that these men and women can easily do in their own cottages so as to supplement their very slender resources? Does any one still doubt that it is only hand-spinning and nothing else? 6

Cottage manufacture of yarn and cloth cannot be expensive even as domestic cookery is not expensive and cannot be replaced by hotel cookery. Over twenty-five crores of the population will be doing their own hand-spinning and having yarn thus manu-factured woven in neighbouring localities. This popu-lation is rooted to the soil, and has at least four months in the year to remain idle.

If they spin during those hours and have the yarn woven and wear it, no mill-made cloth can compete with their Khadi. The cloth thus manufac-tured will be the cheapest possible for them. 7

What is claimed for spinning is that:

1. It supplies the readiest occupation to those who have leisure and are in want of a few coppers;
2. it is known to the thousands;
3. it is easily learnt;

4. it requires practically no outlay of capital;

5. the wheel can be easily and cheaply made. Most of us do not yet know that spinning can be done even with a piece of tile and splinter;

6. the people have no repugnance to it;

7. it affords immediate relief in times of famine and scarcity;

8. it alone can stop the drain of wealth which goes outside India in the purchase of foreign cloth;

9. it automatically distributes the millions thus saved among the deserving poor;

10. even the smallest success means so much immediate gain to the people;

11. it is the most potent instrument of securing co-operation among the people. 8

The disease of the masses is not want of money so much as it is want of work. Labour is money. He who provides dignified labour for the millions in their cottages, provides food and clothing, or which is the same thing, money. The Charkha provides such labour. Till a better substitute is found, it must, therefore, hold the field. 9

Idleness is the great cause, the root of all evil, and if that root can be destroyed, most of the evils can be remedied without further effort. A nation that is starving has little hope or initiative left in it. It becomes indifferent to filth and disease. It says of all reforms, 'to what good?' That winter of despair can only be turned into the 'sun-shine of hope' for the millions only through the life-giving wheel, the Charkha. 10

The spinning wheel is an attempt to produce something out of nothing. If we save sixty crores of rupees to the nation through the spinning wheel, as we certainly can, we add that vast amount to the national income. In the process we automatically organize our villages. And as almost the whole of the amount must be distributed amongst the poorest of the land, it becomes a scheme of just and nearly equal distribution of so much wealth. Add to this immense moral value of such distribution, and the case for the Charkha becomes irresistible. *11*

Indeed, in some places, there are to be found weavers who are classed as untouchables on account of their occupation. They are mostly weavers of coarsest Khadi without any pattern. This class was fast dying out when Khadi came to the rescue and there was created a demand for their coarse manufacture. It was then discovered that there were numerous Harijan families that even subsisted on spinning. Thus Khadi is doubly the poor man's staff of life. It helps the poorest, including the Harijans, who are the most helpless among the poorest. They are so because many occupations which are available to the others are not available to the Harijans. *12*

To those also who aspire to observe Brahma-charya I present the spinning wheel. It is not a thing to be despised, for it is experience here that speaks. A person who wants to subdue his passions has need to be calm. All commotion within him ought to cease; and so quiet and gentle is the motion of the spinning wheel that it has been known to still the passions of those who have turned it in the fullness of faith. . . . Human passions are fleeter even than the wind, and to subdue them completely requires no end of patience. All that I claim is that in the spinning wheel they will find a powerful means of culti-vating steadiness. *13*

Spinning would spell the organization of crores into a joint co-operative effort, the conservation and utilization of the energy of the millions, and the dedication of crores of lives to the service of the motherland. The carrying out of such a gigantic task would, further, give us a realization of our own strength. It would mean our acquiring a thorough mastery of the detail and innumerable knotty problems which it presents, e.g. learning to keep account of every pie, learning to live in the villages in sanitary and healthy conditions, removing the difficulties that block the way and so on. For, unless we learn all this, we would not be able to accomplish this task. The spinning wheel, then, provides us with a means for generating this capacity in us. *14*

The only universal industry for the millions is spinning and no other. That does not mean that other industries do not matter or are useless. Indeed from the individual standpoint any other industry would be more remunerative than spinning. Watch-making will be no doubt a most remunerative and fascinating industry. But how many can engage in it? Is it of any use to the millions of villagers? But if the villagers can reconstruct their home, begin to live again as their forefathers did, if they begin to make good use of their idle hours, all else, all the other industries will revive as a matter of course. *15*

The revival (of Charkha) cannot take place without an army of selfless Indians of intelligence and patriotism working with a single mind in the villages to spread the message of the Charkha and bring a ray of hope and light into their lustreless eyes. This is mighty effort at co-operation and adult education of the correct type. It brings about a silent and sure revolution like the silent but sure and life-giving revolution of the Charkha.

Twenty years' experience of Charkha work has convinced me of the correctness of the argument here advanced by me. The Charkha has served the poor Muslims and Hindus in almost an equal measure. Nearly five crores of rupees have been put into the pockets of these lakhs of village artisans without fuss and tomtoming.

Hence I say without hesitation that the Charkha must lead us to Swaraj in terms of the masses belonging to all faiths. The Charkha restores the villages to their rightful place and abolishes distinctions between high and low. *16*

The spinning wheel is a symbol not of commercial war but of commercial peace. It bears not a message of ill-will towards the nations of the earth but of goodwill and self-help. It will not need the protection of a navy threatening a world's peace and exploiting its resources, but it needs the religious determination of millions to spin their yarn in their own homes as today they cook their food in their own homes. I may deserve the curses of posterity for many mistakes of omission and commission, but I am confident of earning its blessings for suggesting a revival of the Charkha. I stake my all on it. For every revolution of the wheel spins peace, goodwill and love. *17*

It is my claim that (by reviving Khadi and other village industries) we shall have evolved so far that we shall remodel national life in keeping with the ideal of simplicity and domesticity implanted in the bosom of the masses. We will not then be dragged into an imperialism which is built upon exploitation of the weaker races of the earth, and the acceptance of a giddy materialistic civilization protected by naval and air forces that have made peaceful living almost impossible. On the contrary we shall then refine that imperialism into a commonwealth of nations which will combine, if they do, for the purpose of giving their best to the world and of protecting, not by brute force but by self-suffering, the weaker nations or races of the earth. Such a transformation can come only after the complete success of the spinning wheel. India can become fit for delivering such a message, when she has become proof against temptation and therefore attacks from outside, by becoming self-contained regarding two of her chief needs— food and clothing. 18

When once we have revived the one industry (Khadi), all the other industries will follow. I would make the spinning wheel the foundation on which to build a sound village life; I would make the wheel the centre round which all other activities will revolve. 19

The ideal of Khadi has always been as a means, *par excellence*, for the resuscitation of villages and therethrough the generation of real strength among the masses—the strength that will *ipso facto* bring Swaraj. 20

My experience tells me that in order to make Khadi universal both in the cities and villages, it should be made available only in exchange for yarn. As time passes I hope people will themselves insist on buying Khadi through yarn currency. If, however, this does not happen and they produce yarn grudgingly, I fear Swaraj through non-violence will be impossible.

An increase in the number of mills and cities will certainly not contribute to the prosperity of India's millions. On the contrary, it will bring further poverty to the unemployed and all the diseases that follow in the wake of starvation. If town-dwellers can look upon such a spectacle with equanimity there is nothing more to be said. In such an event it will be the reign of violence in India, not a reign of Truth and Ahimsa. And we shall be forced to admit that there is naturally no room there for Khadi. Military training will then have to be compulsory for all. But we must only think in terms of the starving crores. If they are to be restored, if they are to live, then the Charkha must be made the central activity and people must spin voluntarily. *21*

Our work had a very humble beginning. When I started Khadi I had with me, apart from Maganlalbhai and others who had elected to live and die with me, Vitthaldasbhai and a few sisters. We have travelled a long way since then and today about two crores of people have come under the influence of the Charkha. By its help we have been able to provide the village people with a large amount of money. But can we still hold, as we have always maintained, that Swaraj is impossible without the Charkha? So long as we do not substantiate this claim the Charkha is really no more than a measure of relief, to which we turn because we can do nothing else about it. It would not then be the means of our salvation.

Secondly, we have failed to carry our message to the crores of our people. They have neither any knowledge of what the Charkha can do for them nor even the necessary curiosity for it.

The Congress did accept the Charkha. But did it do so willingly? No, it tolerates the Charkha simply for my sake. The Socialists ridicule it outright. They have spoken and written much against it. We have no clear or convincing reply to offer to them. How I wish I could convince them that the Charkha is the key to Swaraj! I have not been able to justify the claim all these years.

Now for my third point: Non-violence is not something of the other world. If it is, I have no use for it. I am of the earth and if non-violence is something really worthwhile I want to realize it here on this earth while still I am alive. And how else can it be realized except in a society which has compassion and other similar virtues as its characteristics?

If you go to the house of one who has use for violence you will find his drawing room decorated with tigers' skins, deers' horns, swords, guns and such like. I have been to the Viceregal Lodge, I also saw Mussolini. In the houses of both I found arms hanging on the walls. I was given a salute with arms, a symbol of violence.

Just as arms symbolize violence the Charkha symbolizes non-violence, in the sense that we can most directly realize non-violence through it. But it cannot symbolize non-violence so long as we do not work in accordance with its spirit. The sword in Mussolini's hall seemed to say " Touch me and I will cut you." It gave a vivid picture of violence. It seemed to ask you to touch it and realize its power. So also we must illustrate the power of the Charkha so that a mere look at it may speak to us about non-violence. But we are bankrupt today. What is our answer to

Socialists? They complain that we have been harping on the Charkha for years and yet we have achieved nothing.

The Charkha was there during Muslim rule also. Dacca was famous for its muslins. The Charkha then was a symbol of poverty and not of non-violence. The kings took forced labour from women and depressed classes. The same was later repeated by the East India Company. Kautilya mentions in his *Arthashastra* the existence of such forced labour. For ages the Charkha was thus a symbol of violence and the use of force and compulsion. The spinner got but a handful of grain or two small coins, while ladies of the court went about luxuriously clad in the finest of muslins, the product of exploited labour.

As against this, I have presented the Charkha to you as a symbol of non-violence. If I did not make it clear to you so far, it was my mistake. You know I am among the maimed and can move but slowly. Yet I do believe that the work done so far has not been a waste.

I shall now pass to my fourth point. We have not yet proved that there can be no Swaraj without the Charkha. It cannot be proved so long as you do not explain it to Congressmen. The Charkha and the Congress should become synonyms.

The task of proving the superiority of non-violence is a difficult one. We have to fathom its depths if we are to realize its truth. The world is going to put me to the test. It may declare me a fool for my tall talk about the Charkha. The task of making the Charkha, which for centuries had been a symbol of poverty, helplessness, injustice and forced labour, the symbol now of mighty non-violent strength, of the new

social order and of the new economy, has fallen on
our shoulders. We have to change history. And I
want to do it through you.

I hope you follow what I am saying. But if in
spite of it you do not believe that the Charkha has the
power to achieve Swaraj, I will ask you to leave me.
Here you are at the cross roads. If you continue with
me without faith you will be deceiving me and doing
a great wrong to the country. I beg of you not to
deceive me in the evening of my life.

It is I who am responsible for defects in our
working so far. The fault is mine because I have
remained the head even when I was conscious of its
defects. But let bygones be bygones. Do we honestly
believe today that the Charkha is the emblem of
non-violence? How many of us are there who believe
so from the depths of our heart?

Now we have the tri-colour flag. What is it but
a piece of Khadi of specific length and breadth? You
can well have another piece in its place. But behind
that Khadi cloth lie encased your feelings. It is a
symbol of Swaraj, a symbol of national emancipation.
We cannot forget it. We will not remove it. We are
prepared to die for it. So also the Charkha should be
an emblem of non-violence.

What does the Charkha, as an emblem of non-
violence, signify in the economic sphere? Call it self-
sufficiency or what you like. In the name of national
reconstruction and self-sufficiency millions are being
bled white in Western countries, as also in other
countries for their sake. Ours is not a self-sufficiency
of that pattern. The Charkha is the way to get rid
of exploitation and domination. I am not so much
concerned with words as with the thing itself.

We are familiar with the controversy in our religion as to whether God has a form or no. The believers in form prefer to worship God through an emblem. So if non-violence is to be pursued as an ideal, the Charkha must be acknowledged as its true form and emblem, and kept ever before view. Whenever I think of non-violence the picture of the Charkha comes before me. We cannot visualize non-violence in the abstract. So we choose an object which can symbolize for us the formless. That is what the Charkha does for me and that is why I worship it. Unless you understand and imbibe this spirit behind my worship of the Charkha you will not gain an understanding of non-violence even for a hundred years. That capacity for non-violence which I find in the Charkha can also be perceived by you only if you approach it with a heart like mine. That is why I say: Follow me or leave me. If you want to come with me I will give you a scheme and do everything possible. If you have not understood what I mean I am prepared to sit and discuss it with you the whole day. But if you say that you have grasped my meaning when you really have not, you will be deceiving both yourselves and me. Ours is not an Association for making profit. We do not seek loaves and fishes. There are a thousand fields in which we can serve the country. Why then remain in Charkha work and sail under false colours? Please do not therefore remain with me under an illusion. Let me go my way alone. But if it were found that I was myself suffering from an illusion and that my belief in the Charkha was mere idol-worship, either you may burn me to ashes with the wood of the Charkha, or I myself would set fire to the Charkha with my own hand.

If the Charkha Sangh has to go, let us wind it up with our own hands. That will put an end to all our struggle. Then the Charkha which has for the moment put us into a labyrinth of difficulties will be left in the hands of a few who believe in it, and may in their hands prove to be a mighty weapon. If you regard it as sheer folly I certainly have no ambition to run an idiots' association and thus degrade the country. On the other hand, if you can manifest non-violence through the Charkha, it will not merely move but sweep forward. You will not then have to worry about keeping it alive.

I repeat that you either leave me alone or digest what I say and follow me. I have brought this new idea to you after two years of penitential thinking. I do not know if I have succeeded in conveying my idea to you. If I have been able to carry conviction please do one thing. Those of you who want to remain with me give me in writing that you regard the Charkha from today as the emblem of non-violence. You have to make your decision today. If you do not or cannot regard the Charkha as the emblem of non-violence and yet you remain with me, then you will thereby put yourself in an awkward plight and also drag me down with you. 22

One epoch of Khadi has ended. Khadi has achieved something for the benefit of the poor. Now we have to demonstrate how the poor can be self-supporting. 23

I saw that our work would be incomplete, so long as we did not carry the message of the Charkha to every home. 24

The Charkha is the symbol of non-violent economic self-sufficiency. If we and the people grasp this significance of the Charkha not a pice need be spent on propaganda for the Charkha. Nor need we look to the rich for alms. We shall without effort become the centre of hope, and the people will come to us of their own accord. They will not go elsewhere to seek work. Every village will become the nerve-centre of independent India. India will then not be known by her cities like Bombay and Calcutta, but by her 400 millions inhabiting the seven lakhs of villages. The problems of Hindu-Muslim differences, untouchability, conflicts, misunderstandings and rivalries will all melt away. This is the real function of the Sangh. We have to live and die for it. *25*

The pursuit of the Charkha must become the mainspring of manifold other activities like village industries, Nai Talim etc. If we are able to adopt the Charkha intelligently we can revive the entire economic life of our villages once more. *26*

By its help we have been able to provide the village people with a large amount of money. But can we still hold, as we have always maintained, that Swaraj is impossible without the Charkha? So long as we do not substantiate this claim the Charkha is really no more than a measure of relief, to which we turn because we can do nothing else about it. It would not then be the means of our salvation. *27*

Now I feel that Khadi alone cannot revive the villages. Village uplift is possible only when we rejuvenate village life as a whole, revive all village industries and make the entire village industrious. *28*

Khadi is not an occupation or draft merely to earn a livelihood. None of us should harbour this idea. *29*

Our reason for putting forward Khadi is that it is the only way to redeem the people from the disease of inertia and indifference, the only way to generate in them the strength for freedom. If other crafts are also thus revitalized, our villages could be made self-sufficient and self-reliant. 30

But what we are required to prove above all is the necessity for Khadi for establishing a strong, non-violent village economy. 31

In my opinion, however, the real celebration (of Charkha Jayanti) will come only when the music of the wheel which is the symbol of Independence and non-violence will be heard in every home. If a few or even a crore of poor women spin in order to earn a pittance, what can the celebration mean to them and what achievement can that be? This can well happen even under a despotic rule and is today visible, wherever capital holds sway. Millionaires are sustained by the charity, they dole out to the poor, may be even in the form of wages.

The celebration will only be truly worth-while when the rich and the poor alike understand that all are equal in the eyes of God, that each one, in his own place, must earn his bread by labour, and that the independence of all will be protected, not by guns and ammunition but by the bullets, in the shape of cones of hand-spun yarn, i.e. not by violence but by non-violence. 32

Ponder and realize what wealth this would mean to India, if 300 crores worth of cloth is produced by their own hands in the villages. This is a veritable mint of gold for them and if Khadi became universal, the villages would rise to unknown heights.

Today our masses are poverty-stricken, without the lustre of hope or intelligence in their eyes. The pure hands of the spinners could create this miracle for them and everyone could help. They should have understanding hearts and seeing eyes to detect the beauty in Khaddar even if it is coarse and not be allured by mill finery which could never clothe their nakedness in the true sense of the term. The only way to clothe their nakedness and drive away hunger is for them to grow their own food and make their own cloth. If this happy consummation could be achieved, the eyes of the whole world would be turned towards India. 33

Before the Charkha class in full swing, everything else appears dull and lifeless to me. For I behold my Rama dancing in every thread drawn. I find Swaraj in it. When I contemplate the strength of the yarn drawn by 40 crores of hands, my heart is filled with an ecstasy of joy. 'O, but 20 crores of Indians will not take to spinning,' you say. Is it not a sign of our ignorance and lack of faith to refuse to believe in the possibility? Is it an impossible thing to expect every one of half the population to spin for an hour a day? If we have not the capacity to sacrifice even this much for our Motherland, what is our love of country worth? 34

CHAPTER 20

OTHER VILLAGE INDUSTRIES

Why Village Industries

I recall a conversation I had with Fazalbhai in 1920 when I was on the eve of launching the movement of Swadeshi. He characteristically said to me, ' If you, Congressmen, become advertising agents of ours, you will do no good to the country except to put a premium on our wares and to raise the prices of our manufactures. His argument was sound. But he was nonplussed when I informed him that I was to encourage hand-spun and hand-woven Khadi which had been woefully neglected and which needed to be revived if the starving and unemployed millions were to be served.

But Khadi is not the only such struggling industry. I therefore suggest to you to direct your attention and effort to all the small-scale, minor, unorganized industries that are today in need of public support. They may be wiped out if no effort is made in their behalf. Some of these are being pushed back by large-scale industries which flood the markets with their manufactures. It is these that cry for your help. *1*

I have no doubt in my mind that we add to the national wealth if we help the small-scale industries. I have no doubt also that true Swadeshi consists in encouraging and reviving these home industries. That alone can help the dumb millions. It also provides an outlet for the creative faculties and resourcefulness of the people. It can also usefully employ hundreds of youths in the country who are in need of employment. It may harness all the energy that at present runs to waste. I do not want any one of those who are engaged in more remunerative occupations to leave them and take to the minor industries. Just as I did with regard to the spinning wheel, I would ask only those who suffer from unemployment and penury to take to some of these industries and add a little to their slender resources.

It will thus be seen that the change in activity that I have suggested to you does in no way conflict with the interests of the major industries. I want to say only this much that you, national servants, will restrict your activities to the minor industries and let the major ones help themselves as they are doing today. The minor industries I conceive will not replace the major ones, but will supplement them. 2

We may profess to gratuitously help textile, sugar and rice mills and, respectively, kill the village spinning wheel, the handloom and their product, Khadi, the village cane-crusher and its product, the vitamin-laden and nourishing *gud* or molasses, and the hand-pounder and its product, unpolished rice, whose pericarp, which holds the vitamins, is left intact by these pounders. Our clear duty is, therefore, to investigate the possibility of keeping in existence the village wheel, the village crusher and the village pounder, and, by advertising their products, discovering their qualities, ascertaining the condition of the workers and the number displaced by the power driven machinery and discovering the methods of improving them, whilst retaining their village character, to enable them to stand the competition of the mills. How terribly and criminally we have neglected them! Here

there is no antagonism to the textile or the sugar
or the rice mills. Their products must be preferred
to the corresponding foreign products. If they were
in danger of extinction from foreign competition, they
should receive the needed support. But they stand
in no such need. They are flourishing in spite of
foreign competition. What is needed is protection
of the village crafts and the workers behind them
from the crushing competition of the power driven
machinery, whether it is worked in India or in foreign
lands. It may be that Khadi, *gud* and unpolished
rice have no intrinsic quality and that they should
die. But, except for Khadi not the slightest effort
has been made, so far as I am aware, to know anything about the fate of the tens of thousands of villagers
who were earning their livelihood through crushing
cane and pounding rice. 3

I have ruled out organized industries, not because
they are *not* Swadeshi, but because they do not need
special support. They can stand on their own legs
and, in the present state of our awakening, can easily
command a market. 4

In a nutshell, of the things we use, we should
restrict our purchases to the articles which villages
manufacture. Their manufactures may be crude.
We must try to induce them to improve their work-
manship, and not dismiss them because foreign articles
or even articles produced in cities, that is big factories,
are superior. In other words, we should evoke the
artistic talent of the villager. In this manner shall we
repay somewhat the debt we owe to them. We need
not be frightened by the thought whether we shall
ever succeed in such an effort. Within our own
times we can recall instances where we have not been

baffled by the difficulty of our tasks when we have known that they were essential for the nation's progress. If, therefore, we as individuals believe that revivification of India's villages is a necessity of our existence, if we believe that thereby only can we root out untouchability and feel one with all, no matter to what community or religion they may belong, we must mentally go back to the villages and treat them as our pattern, instead of putting the city life before them for imitation. If this is the correct attitude, then, naturally, we begin with ourselves and thus use, say, hand-made paper instead of mill-made, use village reed, wherever possible, instead of the fountain pen or the penholder, ink made in the villages instead of the big factories, etc. I can multiply instances of this nature. There is hardly anything of daily use in the home which the villagers have not made before and cannot make even now. If we perform the mental trick and fix our gaze upon them, we immediately put millions of rupees into the pockets of the villagers, whereas at the present moment we are exploiting the villagers without making any return worth the name. It is time we arrested the progress of the tragedy. 5

Bit by bit village people are being confined only to the hand-to-mouth business of scratching the earth. Few know today that agriculture in the small and irregular holdings of India is not a paying proposition. The villagers live a lifeless life. Their life is a process of slow starvation. They are burdened with debts. 6

Extinction of village industries would complete the ruin of the 7,00,000 villages in India. 7

Mechanization is good when the hands are too few for the work intended to be accomplished. It is an evil when there are more hands than required for the work, as is the case in India. 8

But if the cloth manufactured in mills displaces village hands, rice mills and flour mills not only displace thousands of poor women workers, but damage the health of the whole population in the bargain. Where people have no objection to taking flesh diet and can afford it, white flour and polished rice may do no harm, but in India, where millions can get no flesh diet even where they have no objection to eating it if they can get it, it is sinful to deprive them of nutritious and vital elements contained in whole wheat meal and unpolished rice. It is time medical men and others combined to instruct the people on the danger attendant upon the use of white flour and polished rice. 9

The way to take work to the villagers is not through mechanization but through revival of the industries they have hitherto followed. 10

Hence the function of the All India Village Industries Association must, in my opinion, be to encourage the existing industries and to revive, where it is possible and desirable, the dying or dead industries of villages according to the village methods, i.e. the villagers working in their own cottages as they have done from times immemorial. These simple methods can be considerably improved as they have been in hand-ginning, hand-carding, hand-spinning and hand-weaving. 11

Khadi is the sun of the village solar system. The planets are the various industries which can support Khadi in return for the heat and the sustenance they derive from it. Without it, the other industries cannot grow. But during my last tour I discovered that,

without the revival of the other industries, Khadi
could not make further progress. For villagers to be
able to occupy their spare time profitably, the village
must be touched at all points. *12*

Involuntary and voluntary idleness of villagers
make them a perpetual prey of exploiters, foreign and
indigenous. Whether the exploiter is from outside
or from the Indian cities, their state would be the
same, they would have no Swaraj. So I said to
myself, ' Let these people be asked to do something
else; if they will not interest themselves in Khadi,
let them take up some work which used to be done
by their ancestors, but which has of late died out.'
There are numerous things of daily use which they
used to produce themselves not many years ago, but for
which they now depend on the outer world. There
are numerous things of daily use to the town-dweller
for which he depends on the villagers, but which he
now imports from cities. The moment the villagers
decide to devote all their spare time to doing something useful and town-dwellers to use those village
products, the snapped link between the villagers and
the town-dwellers would be restored. *13*

I am not asking the city-dwellers to go to and
live in the villages. But I am asking them to render
unto the villagers what is due to them. Is there any
single raw material that the city-dwellers can obtain
except from the villager? If they cannot, why not
teach him to work on it himself, as he used to before
and as he would do now but for our exploiting in-
roads?*14*

We shall have to see that the villagers become
first of all self-contained and then cater for the needs
of the city-dwellers. *15*

Other village industries come in as a hand-maid to Khadi. They cannot exist without Khadi, and Khadi will be robbed of its dignity without them. Village economy cannot be complete without the essential village industries such as hand-grinding, hand-pounding, soap-making, paper-making, match-making, tanning, oil-pressing, etc. Congressmen can interest themselves in these and, if they are villagers or will settle down in villages, they will give these industries a new life and a new dress. All should make it a point of honour to use only village articles whenever and wherever available. Given the demand there is no doubt that most of our wants can be supplied from our villages. When we have become village-minded, we will not want imitations of the West or machine-made products, but we will develop a true national taste in keeping with the vision of a new India in which pauperism, starvation and idleness will be unknown. *16*

The revival of village industries is but an extension of the Khadi effort. Hand-spun cloth, hand-made paper, hand-pounded rice, home-made bread and jam, are not uncommon in the West. Only there they do not have one-hundredth of the importance they have in India. For, with us, their revival means life, their destruction means death, to the villagers, as he who runs may see. Whatever the machine age may do, it will never give employment to the millions whom the wholesale introduction of power machinery must displace. *17*

All of us should be convinced that the Charkha is the symbol of non-violent economic self-sufficiency. *18*

The pursuit of the Charkha must become the mainspring of manifold other activities like village industries, Nai Talim etc. If we are able to adopt the Charkha intelligently we can revive the entire economic life of our villages once more. *19*

Our worker should be able to identify himself with all that requires to be done in the village, that is, with the entire life of the village and yet feel as light as ever. *20*

I regard Charkha as the centre of village uplift. In addition, the worker will have to see what other village crafts can prosper in his village. The first in order among these crafts will be the bullock oil-press. Our worker would have to know its technique which has now been scientifically improved at Maganwadi. Another industry which may be introduced is hand-made paper. This has to be learnt not with the view of supplying paper to the whole country but in order to make the village self-sufficient and capable of earning a little income.

Next to oil and hand-made paper we must revive tha hand-*chakki* (grinding stone) — a vital thing in every village. Otherwise flour-mills which have been a source of anxiety to me for several years will be our fate. Similarly in regard to rice. We must get our people in the villages to take to hand-pounding of rice or hand-*chakkis* for husking paddy, for it is a well-established fact that the white polished rice put out by mills is harmful to health. *21*

The village worker should acquire all-round knowledge about building up the whole village. There will be some sewing work in the village, smithy, carpentry, leather work, agriculture, etc. The village worker should seek to bring about co-operation among the workers in these various occupations so as to make them serve as harmonious parts of one whole. 22

Now we have to do the work anew with the objective of all-round village uplift. Let us see how far we can go. Even if our present activities have to be slackened or reduced to nought for sometime on account of these changes, it does not matter. We have created some sentiment about Khadi among the people. But if there is some error in what we told the people about the significance of Khadi we must pause. If ours was a wrong claim we must declare our error openly and withdraw our claim.

I would ask city-dwellers to produce their own Khadi. I would forgo the temptation to supply Khadi to them. We shall go and settle in the villages. In case workers want to leave us on account of this change we shall let them go. Unless our head and heart are converted to this extent we cannot achieve the desired result. We of the A.I.S.A. will merely direct policy. But decentralizing our work as much as possible we shall free ourselves from day to day Khadi work completely. Thereafter we shall concentrate our energy and attention on the other activities or crafts carried out in the vicinity of the village we settle in. Only then will the real substance of our work be realized. . . . Today our main concern should be to lay the foundation for this work as deep as possible. 23

I am thinking of ways and means of improving the condition of the people through a rehabilitation of agriculture, cattle-breeding and all other village industries. My problem will be solved, if I succeed even in half a dozen villages, for as is the part so is the whole. 24

Begin with Yourself

Correspondents have been writing, and friends have been seeing me, to ask me how to begin the village industries work and what to do first.

The obvious answer is, "Begin with yourself and do first that which is easiest for you to do."

This answer, however, does not satisfy the enquirers. Let me, therefore, be more explicit.

Each person can examine all the articles of food, clothing and other things that he uses from day to day and replace foreign makes or city makes, by those produced by the villagers in their homes or fields with the simple inexpensive tools they can easily handle and mend. This replacement will be itself, an education of great value and a solid beginning. The next step will be opened out to him of itself. For instance, say, the beginner has been hitherto using a tooth-brush made in a Bombay factory. He wants to replace it with a village brush. He is advised to use a *babul* twig. If he has weak teeth or is toothless, he has to crush one end of it, with a rounded stone or a hammer, on a hard surface. The other end he slits with a knife and uses the halves as tongue-scrapers. He will find these brushes to be cheaper and much cleaner than the very unhygienic factory-made tooth-brush. The city-made tooth-powder he naturally replaces with equal parts of clean, finely-ground, wood-charcoal and clean salt. He will replace mill-cloth with village-spun Khadi, and mill-husked rice with hand-husked, unpolished rice, and white sugar with village-made *gur*. These I have taken merely as samples . . . to deal with the difficulties that have been mentioned by those who have been discussing the question with me. 25

Dairying

Criminal negligence is the only cause of the miserable condition of our cattle. Our *pinjrapoles*, though they are an answer to our instinct for mercy, are a clumsy demonstration of its execution. Instead of being model dairy farms and great profitable national institutions, they are merely depots for receiving decrepit cattle. Whilst professing the religion of cow protection, we have enslaved the cow and her progeny, and have become slaves ourselves. 26

An ideal *goshala* would supply the city of its domicile with cheap and wholesome milk from cattle of its own keeping, and cheap and lasting foot-wear not out of slaughtered hide but of the hide of dead cattle. Such a *goshala* will not be on one or two acres of ground in the heart of a city or in its immediate neighbourhood but it would have at some distance, but within easy reach, fifty to a hundred acres of ground where a modern dairy and a modern tannery would be conducted on strictly business but national lines. Thus there would be no profits and no dividends to be paid and there would be also no loss incurred. In the long run such institutions dotted all over India would be a triumph of Hinduism and would be proof of Hindu earnestness about cow, that is, cattle protection and it would provide decent employment for thousands of men including educated men; for both dairy and tannery work requires expert scientific knowledge. Not Denmark but Indian should be a model State for the finest dairy experiments, and India should not to her shame have to export nine crore rupees worth of dead cattle hide annually and for her consumption use slaughtered cattle hide.

If such a state of things is a shame for India it is a greater shame for Hindus. I wish that all the *goshala* Committees will take to heart the remarks I made in reply to the Giridih address and make their *goshalas* into ideal dairies and tanneries and a refuge for all worn out and maimed cattle. 27

Every *goshala* or *pinjrapole* should have a tannery adequate to its needs attached to it. In other words, the manager in charge of every such institution should have a thorough knowledge of the immediate steps necessary for utilizing the remains of dead cattle. If this is done, the question, viz. how many heads of cattle should a particular *goshala* contain, would not arise at all.

I do not know what the rate of mortality of cattle in *goshalas* is nor is it relevant to my proposition. So long as there is a single head of cattle in a *goshala* its manager ought to know how to dispose of its remains after it is dead, just as he is expected to know how to look after it while it is alive.

Such humanitarian institutions for the protection of cattle as I have described should normally take charge of the remains of the cattle that might die in the village. Therein lies the interest of the cattle, the depressed classes and the general public alike. In villages where there are no *goshalas* or the concomitant tanneries, some local person who believes in cow protection should take it upon himself to get the carcasses removed to the nearest tannery or get the preliminary processes performed upon it and send the useful parts there.

The establishment of such tanneries as I have described does not require much capital outlay. Only some initial expenditure would be needed to train up workers for this work. 28

Hand-pounding of Rice and Hand-grinding of Corn

In my writing on cent per cent Swadeshi, I have shown how some aspects of it can be tackled immediately with benefit to the starving millions both economically and hygienically. The richest in the land can share the benefit. Thus if rice can be pounded in the villages after the old fashion, the wages will fill the pockets of the rice-pounding sisters and the rice-eating millions will get some sustenance from the unpolished rice instead of pure starch which the polished rice provides. Human greed, which takes no account of the health or the wealth of the people who come under its heels, is responsible for the hideous rice-mills one sees in all the rice-producing tracts. If public opinion was strong, it will make rice-mills an impossibility by simply insisting on unpolished rice and appealing to the owners of rice-mills to stop a traffic that undermines the health of a whole nation and robs the poor people of an honest means of livelihood. 29

I regard the existence of power wheels for the grinding of corn in thousands of villages as the limit of our helplessness. I suppose India does not produce all the engines or grinding machines. . . . The planting of such machinery and engines on a large scale in villages is also a sign of greed. Is it proper to fill one's pockets in this manner at the expense of the poor? Every such machinery puts thousands of hand-*chakkis* out of work and takes away

employment from thousands of housewives and artisans who make these *chakkis*. Moreover, the process
is infective and will spread to every village industry.
The decay of the latter spells too the decay of art.
If it meant replacement of old crafts by new ones,
one might not have much to say against it. But this is
not what is happening. In the thousands of villages
where power machinery exists, one misses the sweet
music in the early morning of the grinders at
work. *30*

Machine Oil and Ghani Oil

Shri Jhaverbhai has also examined the cause of
the decline of the village *ghani*. The most potent
cause is the inability of the oilman to command a
regular supply of seeds. The villages are practically
deluded of seeds after the season. The oilman has no
money to store the seeds, much less to buy them in
the cities. Therefore he has disappeared or is fast
disappearing. Lakhs of *ghanis* are today lying idle
causing a tremendous waste of the country's resources. Surely it is the function of the State to resuscitate the existing *ghanis* by conserving seeds in the
places of their origin and making them available to
the village oilman at reasonable rates. The Government loses nothing by giving this aid. It can be given,
so Shri Jhaverbhai contends, through co-operative
societies or Panchayats. If this is done, Shri Jhaverbhai is of opinion, based on research, that *ghani* oil
can compete with the machine product and villager
can be spared the infliction of the adulterated oil he
gets today. It should be borne in mind that the only
fat the villager gets, when he gets any, is what the
oils can give him. To *ghee* he is generally a stranger.

He (Shri Jhaverbhai) has found out why this machine oil is at all cheaper than the *ghani* oil. He gives three reasons, two of which are unavoidable. They are capital and the ability of the machine to extract the last drop of oil and that too in a shorter time than the *ghani*. These advantages are neutralized by the commission the owner of this oil mill has to pay to the middleman. But Shri Jhaverbhai cannot cope with the third reason, adulteration, unless he also takes to it. This naturally he will not do. He therefore suggests that adulteration should be dealt with by the law. This can be done by enforcing the Anti-Adulteration Act if there is one or by enacting it by licensing oil mills. *31*

Gur and Khandsari

Take the sugar industry. The largest major industry next to the textile is that of the manufacture of sugar. It stands in no need of our assistance. Sugar factories are fast multiplying. Popular agencies have done little to help the growth of this industry. It is indebted for its growth to favourable legislation. And today the industry is so prosperous and expanding that the production of jaggery is becoming a thing of the past. It is admittedly superior to refined sugar in nutritive value. It is this very valuable cottage industry that cries out for your help. This by itself furnishes large scope for research and substantial help. We have to investigate the ways and means of keeping it alive. This is but an illustration of what I mean. *32*

The advantages, attributed to *tadi*, are all available from other foodstuffs. *Tadi* is made out of *khajuri* juice. Fresh *khajuri* juice is not an intoxicant.

It is known as *nira* in Hindustani and many people have been cured of their constipation as a result of drinking *nira*. I have taken it myself though it did not act as a laxative with me. I found that it had the same food value as sugar-cane juice. If one drinks a glass of *nira* in the morning instead of drinking tea etc., he should not need anything else for breakfast. As in the sugar-cane juice, palm juice can be boiled to make palm jaggery. *Khajuri* is a variety of palm tree. Several varieties of palm grow spontaneously in our country. All of them yield drinkable juice. As *nira* gets fermented very quickly, it has to be used up immediately and therefore on the spot. Since this condition is difficult to fulfil except to a limited extent, in practice, the best use of *nira* is to convert it into palm jaggery. Palm jaggery can well replace sugar-cane jaggery. In fact some people prefer it to the latter. One advantage of palm jaggery over sugar-cane jaggery is that it is less sweet and therefore one can eat more of it. The All-India Village Industries Association has done a great deal to popularize palm jaggery, but much remains to be done. If the palms that are used for making *tadi* are used for making jaggery, India will never lack sugar and the poor will be able to get good jaggery for very little money. Palm jaggery can be converted into molasses and refined sugar. But the jaggery is much more useful than refined sugar. The salts present in the jaggery are lost in the process of refining. Just as refined wheat flour and polished rice lose some of their nutritive value because of the loss of the pericarp, refined sugar also loses some of the nutritive value of the jaggery. One may generalize that all foodstuffs are richer if taken in their natural state as far as possible.*33*

Bee-keeping

Bee-keeping seems to me to possess immense possibilities. Apart from its village value, it may be cultivated as a hobby by moneyed young men and women. They will add to the wealth of the country and produce the finest health-giving sugar for themselves. If they are philanthropically inclined, they can distribute it as health-giving food among sickly Harijan children. There is no reason why it should be a luxury of the rich or an expensive medicinal vehicle in the hands of the *hakims* and *vaidyas*. No doubt, my hope is based on inferences drawn from meagre data. Experiments that may be made in villages and in cities by young men and women should show whether honey can become a common article of food or has to remain an uncommon article, which it is today. *34*

Tanning

It is estimated that rupees nine crores worth of raw hide is annually exported from India and that much of it is returned to her in the shape of manufactured articles. This means not only a material, but also an intellectual, drain. We miss the training we should receive in tanning and preparing the innumerable articles of leather we need for daily use.

Tanning requires great technical skill. An army of chemists can find scope for their inventive talent in this great industry. There are two ways of developing. One for the uplift of Harijans living in the villages and eking out a bare sustenance, living in filth and degradation and consigned to the village ghetto, isolated and away from the village proper. This way means part re-organization of villages and taking art, education, cleanliness, prosperity and dignity to them. This means also the application of chemical talent to village uplift. Tanning chemists have to discover improved methods of tanning. The village chemist has to stoop to conquer. He has to learn and understand the crude village tanning, which is still in existence but which is fast dying owing to neglect, not to say want of support. But the crude method may not be summarily scrapped, at least not before a sympathetic examination. It has served well for centuries. It could not have done so, if it had no merit. The only research I know in this direction is being carried on in Santiniketan, and then it was started at the now defunct Ashram at Sabarmati. I have not been able to keep myself in touch with the progress of the experiment at Santiniketan. There is every prospect of its revival at the Harijan Ashram, which the Sabarmati Ashram has now become. These experiments are mere drops in the ocean of possible research.

Cow-preservation is an article of faith in Hinduism. No Harijan worth his salt will kill cattle for food. But, having become untouchable, he has learnt the evil habit of eating carrion. He will not kill a cow but will eat with the greatest relish the flesh of a dead cow. It may be physiologically harmless. But psychologically there is nothing, perhaps, so repulsive as carrion-eating. And yet, when a dead cow is brought to a Harijan tanner's house, it is a day of rejoicing for the whole household. Children dance round the carcass, and as the animal is flayed, they take hold of bones or pieces of flesh and throw them at one another. As a tanner, who is living at the Harijan Ashram, describing the scenes at his own now forsaken home, tells me the whole family is drunk with joy at the sight of the dead animal. I know how hard I have found it working among Harijans to wean them from the soul-destroying habit of eating carrion. Reformed tanning means the automatic disappearance of carrion-eating.

Well, here is the use for high intelligence and the art of dissection. Here is also a mighty step in the direction of cow-preservation. The cow must die at the hands of the butcher, unless we learn the art of increasing her capacity of milk-giving, unless we improve her stock and make her male progeny more useful for the field and carrying burdens, unless we make scientific use of all her excreta as manure, and unless, when she and hers die, we are prepared to make the wisest use of her hide, bone, flesh, entrails, etc.

I am just now concerned only with the carcass. It is well to remember here that the village tanner, thank God, has to deal only with the carcass, not the slaughtered animal. He has no means of bringing the dead animal in a decent way. He lifts it, drags it, and this injures the skin and reduces the value of the hide. If the villagers and the public knew the priceless and noble service the tanner renders, they will provide easy and simple methods of carrying it, so as not to injure the skin at all.

The next process is flaying the animal. This requires great skill. I am told that none, not even surgeons, do this work better or more expeditiously than the village tanner does with his village knife. I have inquired of those who should know. They have not been able to show me an improvement upon the village tanner. This is not to say that there is none better. I merely give the reader the benefit of my own very limited experience. The village tanner has no use for the bone. He throws it away. Dogs hover round the carcass whilst it is flayed, and take away some, if not all, of the bones. This is a dead loss to the country. The bones, if powdered fine, apart from their other uses, make valuable manure. What remains after the dogs have taken away their share is transported to foreign countries and returns to us in the shape of handles, buttons, etc.

The second way is urbanizing this great industry. There are several tanneries in India doing this work. Their examination is outside the scope of this article. This urbanization can do little good to the Harijans, much less to the villages. It is a process of double drain from the villages. Urbanization in India is slow but sure death for her villages and villagers. Urbanization can never support ninety per cent of India's population, which is living in her 7,00,000 villages. To remove from these villages tanning and such other industries is to remove what little opportunity there still is for making skilled use of the hand and the head. And when the village handicrafts disappear, the villagers working only with their cattle on the field, with idleness for six or four months in the year, must, in the words of Madhusudan Das, be reduced to the level of the beast and be without proper nourishment, either of the mind or the body, and, therefore, without joy and without hope.

Here is work for the cent per cent Swadeshi lover and scope for the harnessing of technical skill to the solution of a great problem. The work fells three apples with one throw. It serves the Harijans,

it serves the villagers, and it means honourable
employment for the middle class intelligentsia who are
in search of employment. Add to this the fact that
intelligentsia have a proper opportunity of coming
in direct touch with the villagers. 35

Soap

Villages would prepare their own soap from
sajji-clay. That soap will not have the luring frag-
rance of soaps turned out in the factories of Tata
and Godrej. Its packing also will not be so attractive.
But it will have the quality of self-sufficiency even
like Khadi. 36

Hand-made Paper

I was told that, if there were enough orders,
the paper could be supplied at the same cost as the
mill-made article. I know that hand-made paper
can never supply the daily growing demand for
paper. But lovers of the seven hundred thousand
villages and their handicrafts will always want to
use hand-made paper, if it is easily procurable.
Those who use hand-made paper know that it
has a charm of its own. Who does not know the famous
Ahmedabad paper? What mill-made paper can
beat it in durability or polish?

The account-books of the old style are still made
of that paper. But it is probably a perishing industry
like many such others. With a little encouragement,
it ought never to perish. If there was supervision,
the processes might be improved and the defects that
are to be noticed with some of this hand-made paper
may be easily removed. The economic condition of

the numberless people engaged in these little known trades is well worth investigating. They will surely allow themselves to be guided and advised and feel thankful to those who would take interest in them.37

Ink

The ink with which I am writing comes from Tenali. It supports about 12 workers. It is making headway against odds. I had three more specimens sent to me by different makers, all no doubt struggling like the Tenali group. They interested me. I entered into correspondence with them. But I could do no more for them. A Swadeshi organization will examine the samples of these inks in a scientific manner and guide them and encourage the most promising ones. It is a good and growing industry requiring expert chemical knowledge. 38

Village Exhibitions

If we want and believe that the village should not only survive but also become strong and flourishing, then the village perspective is the only correct view-point. If this is true then in our exhibitions there can be no place for the glamour and pomp of the cities. There should be no necessity for games and other entertainments that belong to the cities. An exhibition should not become a *tamasha*; nor a source of income; it should never become the advertising medium for traders. No sales should be allowed there. Even Khadi and village industry products should not be sold. An exhibition should be a medium of education, should be attractive and it should be such as to infuse in the villager the impulse to take to some industry or the other. It should bring out the glaring defects and drawbacks in the present day village life, and show methods to be adopted to set them right. It should also be able to indicate the extent of achievement in that direction ever since the idea of village uplift was sponsored. It should also teach how to make village life artistic.

Now let us see what an exhibition will be like if it is to conform to the above conditions.

1. There should be two models of villages— one as existing today and the other an improved one. The improved village will be clean all throughout. Its houses, its roads, its surroundings and its fields will be all clean. The condition of the cattle should also improve. Books, charts, and pictures should be used to show what industries give increased income and how.

2. It must show how to conduct the various village industries, wherefrom to obtain the needed implements, how to make them. The actual working of each industry should be demonstrated. Along with these the following should also find place:

(a) Ideal village diet;

(b) Comparison between village industry and machine industry;

(c) Model lessons on rearing animals;

(d) Art section;

(e) Model of village latrine;

(f) Farm-yard manure, v. chemical manure;

(g) Utilization of hides, bones, etc. of animals;

(h) Village music, musical instruments, village dramas;

(i) Village games, village *akhadas* and forms of exercise;

(j) Nai Talim;

(k) Village medicine;

(l) Village maternity home.

Subject to the policy enunciated in the beginning, this list may be further expanded. What I have indicated is by way of example only, it should not be taken to be exhaustive. I have not made any mention of the Charkha and other village industries as they are taken for granted. Without them the exhibition will be absolutely useless. 39

CHAPTER 21

VILLAGE TRANSPORT

A Plea for the Village Cart

Shri Ishvarbhai S. Amin of Baroda sends me a long note on animal power *v.* machine power. From it I copy the following relevant portion:

"Animal power is not costlier than machine power in fields or short distance work and hence can compete with the latter in most cases. The present-day tendency is towards discarding animal power in preference to machine power.

Take for example a bullock-driven cart, costing Rs. 100 and Rs. 200 for the bullocks. The bullocks can drive the cart at least 15 miles per day with a load of 16 Bengal maunds on rough sandy village roads. This service will cost Re 0-12-0 for two bullocks, Re 0-6-0 for the cartman and Re 0-4-0 for cart depreciation, in total Re 1-6-0 per day. A one-ton motor lorry will cost for 15 miles at least one gallon of petrol, some lubricating oil, huge repair and upkeep expenses, and a costly driver. For 15 miles' run the lorry will cost Re 1-12-0 for petrol including lubricating oil,

Re 0-12-0 for maintenance at the rate of Rs 6 per day of eight hours' service and Re 0-8-0 for the driver, cleaner and extra men required to load and empty the lorry. Hence the total cost is Rs 2-12-0 i.e. Re 1-6-0 per cartload of 16 Bengal maunds. One bullock cart is able to carry 7 to 8 cartloads of manure in one day from the village site to the field which is about ½ mile away and will cost only Re 1-6-0 plus Re 0-6-0 for the extra man required to help the cartman to fill and empty the cart. While a motor lorry to do this job will not cost in any way less. A motor lorry may compete when it has to carry loads at a stretch for a long distance on a good metal road, where bullock carts seem too slow and uneconomical. It is also not desirable to take animals long distances at one stretch as it tells much upon their energy and strength. Bullock carts, however, have been found toiling long distances all day and night in competition with motor lorries from railway stations to far-off interior places, but the physical condition of these bullocks is pitiable, because the owners give them less food in proportion to the low earning. It is the slowness only which goes against the bullock cart, when rapid transport of goods or the movement of men from one place to another is considered important. Villagers, however, to whom spare time brings no money and time saved by motor is of no importance, should make it a point to walk for short distances and use carts for long journeys. If a farmer has his own cart and travels in it, he has not to spend anything in the form of ready money but uses the produce of his own field in producing power by feeding bullocks. Really grass and grain should be looked upon by the farmer as his petrol, and the cart the motor lorry, and bullocks the engine converting grass into power. The machine will neither consume grass nor will it yield manure, an article of vast importance. Then the villager has to have his bullocks; in any case he has his grass. And if he has a cart, he is maintaining the village carpenter and the blacksmith; and if he is keeping a cow, he is maintaining a hydrogenation plant converting vegetable oil into solid butter or ghee and also at the same time a bullock manufacturing machine—thus serving a twofold purpose."

The invasion of the motor lorry may or may not succeed. It would be wisdom if intelligent workers will study the pros and cons and definitely guide the villagers. Shri Ishvarbhai's note should provoke the thought of all village workers in the direction indicated in it. *1*

Motor *V.* Cart

Gram Udyog Patrika for August (1946) examines the respective merits of motor vans and carts for village propaganda. Those who will read the whole argument should send for the *Patrika*. I give below the most important part of the argument:

"We have been asked whether District Boards and other such local bodies, who wish to set apart a certain amount of money for village work will do well to invest in motor vans for propaganda work of various kinds in villages. It is a happy sign that institutions such as these are beginning to realize their duty to the villages and are seeking to bridge the gulf that now exists between towns and villages and between the literate and the illiterate. The question is whether speeding up matters by the use of motor vans which can visit more than one village in a night will suit the purpose.

In all our expenditure, especially when that expenditure is undertaken expressly for the benefit of the village people, it is necessary to see that the money spent goes back to the villager. District and Local Boards obtain their money from the people, and their purchases must be such as will help to circulate money among the people. If on the other hand the money taken from the villagers by way of rates and taxes is sent out of the locality, it must necessarily result in impoverishment of the people, and this will perforce mean that there will be less and less money in the coffers of District and Local Boards.

A Local Board does not set apart more than a few thousands of rupees for village work. If it decides to buy even one motor van for the purpose, it means about Rs 5,000 sent out of the locality to pay for the van and, in addition, constant expenditure on tyres and other spare parts, besides day to day expenditure on petrol, all of which are imported and to pay for which money has to be drained out of the locality. The manifest object of this expenditure is rural welfare, but, in order to be able to hear occasional lectures on agriculture, health, prohibition, child welfare and such like, or to listen to the gramophone or the radio, the villager has to bear this heavy expenditure when he and his family have to live on about Rs 2 a month. What the villager needs above all is profitable employment. We steadily deprive him of employment by buying imported articles, and by way of compensation give him lectures, magic lantern shows and tinned music all at his expense, and pat oursleves on the back that we are working for his welfare. Can anything be more absurd?

Compare with this what happens if in the place of the motor van the much despised bullock cart were used. It will not make so much stir nor so effectively declare to all the world that something wonderful is being done for the villages. But if mere stage-acting and trumpet-blowing are not intended but real quiet constructive work, then we submit that the bullock cart will do much better. It can reach the most remote villages which a motor lorry cannot do.

It costs only a fraction of the money required for a van, so that many bullock carts can be bought, if necessary, to serve groups of villages in the district. The money spent on them goes to the village carpenter, blacksmith and cart-driver. Not a pie of it need go out of the district. The cart itself may be made an exhibit if it is scientifically constructed with disked wheels, proper steel bearings, and axles with well placed and designed hubs, spokes and felloes. The expenditure on equipment consequently instead of draining wealth out of the village will direct it into it. A motor is necessary where speed is of the essence of the work to be done. But nothing of the kind can be claimed for propaganda to be carried on in villages for rural welfare. On the other hand, slow, steady methods will be of greater avail. It will be an advantage not to be able to rush from one village to another but to spend some time in each place. Only thus can the life and the problems of the people be properly understood, and the work directed to meet those problems be effective.

Rural work and motor vans appear, therefore to go ill together. What is required is steady, constructive effort, not lightning speed and empty show. We would commend to Local Boards and public institutions genuinely interested in village welfare to start by using only village-made goods, to study the conditions which are steadily producing poverty in the villages, and concentrate on removing them one by one. When every side of village life needs intensive, well-considered effort, it seems a waste of public money to throw it away on methods which attempt to bring about village up-lift overnight."

It is to be hoped that those who interest themselves in village welfare will take to heart the obvious argument advanced in favour of the cart. It will be cruel to destroy the village economy through the very agency designed for village welfare. 2

Bullocks as Means of Transport

The bullocks are the means of transport everywhere in our villages and have not ceased to be such even in a place like Simla. The railway train and the motor car go there, but all along the mountain road I found bullocks trudging up and down dragging heavily-laden carts. It seems as if this means of transport is part of our lives and our civilization. And the bullock has to endure if our handicraft civilization is to endure.

You have to find out whose animals are the best and to discover how he manages to keep them so well. You will find out whose cow gives the largest amount of milk and discover how he keeps her and feeds her. You may fix some prize for the best bullock and the best cow in the village. Without model cattle we cannot have a model village. 3

CHAPTER 22

CURRENCY, EXCHANGE AND TAX

Under my system, it is labour which is the current coin, not metal. Any person who can use his labour has that coin, has wealth. He converts his labour into cloth, he converts his labour into grain. If he wants peraffin oil, which he cannot himself produce, he uses his surplus grain for getting the oil. It is exchange of labour on free, fair and equal terms—hence it is no robbery. You may object that this is a reversion to the primitive system of barter. But is not all international trade based on the barter system? *1*

Then every village of India will almost be a self-supporting and self-contained unit, exchanging only such necessary commodities with other villages where they are not locally producible. *2*

My experience tells me that in order to make Khadi universal both in the cities and villages, it should be made available only in exchange for yarn. As time passes I hope people will themselves insist on buying Khadi through yarn currency. *3*

Labour, as a matter of fact, is as much money as metallic coin. If some put their money in any particular concern, you put your labour in it. Just as without money your labour would be useless, so also the money in the world would be perfectly useless without labour. *4*

Self-sufficiency does not mean narrowness. To be self-sufficient is not to be altogether self-contained. In no circumstances would we be able to produce all the things we need. So though our aim is complete self-sufficiency, we shall have to get from outside the village what we cannot produce in the village; we shall have to produce more of what we can in order thereby to obtain in exchange what we are unable to produce. *5*

Just as gold and silver emerge as coin from the mint, so Khadi alone should emerge from a yarn bank. *6*

In my part of India shells and seedless dried almonds were used as coins accepted by the people and the State treasury. They had no intrinsic value. They were measure of people's deep poverty. They could not afford the lowest metal coin. Five shells would buy them a little vegetable or a needle. I have suggested a measure which will not be a mere token but which will have always an intrinsic value which will also be its market value. In that sense it will be an ideal measure. For the present and by way of experiment I have suggested a warp length of a single thread of yarn as the lowest measure and to be used in dealings principally with the spinners and generally with Khadi-lovers. The spinners can have all their daily wants supplied as against fixed quantity of yarn. Stores will need to be maintained by the A.I.S.A. in combination with the A.I.V.I.A. and ultimately with those who will give their co-operation. As I conceive it, the system can be worked only if it is decentralized. This is not its demerit but merit.7

Payment (of tax) in labour invigorates the nation. Where people perform labour voluntarily for the service of society, exchange of money becomes unnecessary. The labour of collecting the taxes and keeping accounts is saved and the results are equally good.8

CHAPTER 23

VILLAGE SANITATION

Divorce between intelligence and labour has resulted in criminal negligence of the villages. And so, instead of having graceful hamlets dotting the land, we have dung-heaps. The approach to many villages is not a refreshing experience. Often one would like to shut one's eyes and stuff one's nose; such is the surrounding dirt and offending smell. If the majority of Congressmen were derived from our villages, as they should be, they should be able to make our villages models of cleanliness in every sense of the word. But they have never considered it their duty to identify themselves with the villagers in their daily lives. A sense of national or social sanitation is not a virtue among us. We may take a kind of a bath, but we do not mind dirtying the well or the tank or the river by whose side or in which we perform ablutions. I regard this defect as a great vice which is responsible for the disgraceful state of our villages and the sacred banks of the sacred rivers and for the diseases that spring from insanitation. 1

The things to attend to in the villages are cleaning tanks and wells and keeping them clean, getting rid of dung heaps. If the workers will begin the work themselves, working like paid *bhangis* from day to day and always letting the villagers know that they are expected to join them so as ultimately to do the whole work themselves, they may be sure that they will find that the villagers will sooner or later co-operate.

Lanes and streets have to be cleansed of all the rubbish, which should be classified. There are portions which can be turned into manure, portions which have simply to be buried and portions which can be directly turned into wealth. Every bone picked up is valuable raw material from which useful articles can be made or which can be crushed into rich manure. Rags and waste-paper can be turned into paper, and excreta picked up are golden manure for the village fields.

Village tanks are promiscuously used for bathing, washing clothes, and drinking and cooking purposes. Many village tanks are also used by cattle. Buffaloes are often to be seen wallowing in them. The wonder is that, in spite of this sinful misuse of village tanks, villages have not been destroyed by epidemics. It is the universal medical evidence that this neglect to ensure purity of the water supply of villages is responsible for many of the diseases suffered by the villagers.

This, it will be admitted, is a gloriously interesting and instructive service, fraught with incalculable benefit to the suffering humanity of India. I hope it is clear from my description of the way in which the problem should be tackled, that, given willing workers who will wield the broom and the shovel with the same ease and pride as the pen and the pencil, the question of expense is almost wholly eliminated. All the outlay that will be required is confined to a broom, a basket, a shovel and a pickaxe, and possibly some disinfectant. Dry ashes are, perhaps, as effective a disinfectant as any that a chemist can supply. But here let philanthropic chemists tell us what is the most effective and cheap

village disinfectant that villagers can improvise in
their villages. 2

CHAPTER 24

VILLAGE HEALTH AND HYGIENE

In a well-ordered society the citizens know and
observe the laws of health and hygiene. It is established beyond doubt that ignorance and neglect
of the laws of health and hygiene are responsible for
the majority of diseases to which mankind is heir.
The very high death rate among us is no doubt due
largely to our gnawing poverty, but it could be miti-
gated if the people were properly educated about
health and hygiene.

Mens sana in corpore sano is perhaps the first law
for humanity. A healthy mind in a healthy body is a
self-evident truth. There is an inevitable connection
between mind and body. If we were in possession of
healthy minds, we would shed all violence and,
naturally obeying the laws of health, we would have
healthy bodies without an effort.[1]

It is necessary to understand the meaning of the
word health. Health means body ease. He is a healthy
man whose body is free from all disease; he carries
on his normal activities without fatigue. Such a man
should be able with ease to walk ten to twelve miles
a day, and perform ordinary physical labour without getting tired. He can digest ordinary simple
food. His mind and his senses are in a state of harmony
and poise.[2]

The fundamental laws of health and hygiene are simple and easily learnt. The difficulty is about their observance. Here are some:

Think the purest thoughts and banish all idle and impure thoughts.

Breathe the freshest air day and night.

Establish a balance between bodily and mental work.

Stand erect, sit erect, and be neat and clean in every one of your acts, and let these be an expression of your inner condition.

Eat to live for service of fellow-men. Do not live for indulging yourselves. Hence your food must be just enough to keep your mind and body in good order. Man becomes what he eats.

Your water, food and air must be clean, and you will not be satisfied with mere personal cleanliness, but you will infect your surroundings with the same threefold cleanliness that you will desire for yourselves. 3

Nature Cure for Disease

The practice of nature cure does not require high academic qualifications or much erudition. Simplicity is the essence of universality. Nothing that is meant for the benefit of the millions requires much erudition. The latter can be acquired only by the few and therefore can benefit the rich only. But India lives in her seven lakhs of villages—obscure, tiny, out-of-the-way villages, where the population in some cases hardly exceeds a few hundred, very often not even a few score. I would like to go and settle down in some such village. That is real India, my India, for which I live. You cannot take to these humble people the paraphernalia of highly qualified doctors and hospital equipment. In simple natural remedies and Ramanama lies their only hope. *4*

I hold that where the rules of personal, domestic and public sanitation are strictly observed and due care is taken in the matter of diet and exercise, there should be no occasion for illness or disease. Where there is absolute purity, inner and outer, illness becomes impossible. If the village people could but understand this, they would not need doctors, *hakims* or *vaidyas*.

Nature cure implies an ideal mode of life and that in its turn presupposes ideal living conditions in towns and villages. The name of God is, of course, the hub round which the nature cure system revolves. *5*

Nature cure implies that the treatment should be the cheapest and the simplest possible. The ideal is that such treatment should be carried out in the villages. The villagers should be able to provide the necessary means and equipment. What cannot be had in the villages should be procured. Nature cure does mean a change for the better in one's outlook on life itself. It means regulation of one's life in accordance with the laws of health. It is not a matter of taking the free medicine from the hospital or for fees. A man who takes free treatment from the hospital accepts charity. The man who accepts nature cure never begs. Self-help enhances self-respect. He takes steps to cure himself by eliminating poisons from the system and takes precautions against falling ill in the future.

Right diet and balanced diet are necessary. Today our villages are as bankrupt as we are ourselves.

To produce enough vegetables, fruits and milk in the villages, is an essential part of the nature cure scheme. Time spent on this should not be considered a waste. It is bound to benefit all the villagers and ultimately the whole of India. 6

The nature cure of my conception for the villagers is limited to rendering such aid as can be given to them through what can be procured in the village. For example, I would not need either electricity or ice for them. Such work can only be for those like me who have become village-minded. 7

My nature cure is designed solely for villagers and villages. Therefore, there is no place in it for the microscope, X-rays and similar things. Nor is there room in nature cure for medicines, such as quinine, emetin and penicillin. Personal hygiene and healthy living are of primary importance. And these should suffice. If everyone could achieve perfection in this art, there could be no disease. And, while obeying all the laws of nature in order to cure illness, if it does come, the sovereign remedy ever lies in Ramanama. But this cure through Ramanama cannot become universal in the twinkling of an eye. To carry conviction to the patient, the physician has to be a living embodiment of the power of Ramanama. Meantime, all that can possibly be had from the five agencies of nature must be taken and used. They are earth, water, ether, fire and wind. This, to my mind, is the limit of nature cure. Therefore, my experiment in Uruli Kanchan consists in teaching the villagers how to live clean and healthy lives and in trying to cure the sick through the proper use of the five agencies. If necessary, curative herbs that grow locally, may be used. Wholesome and balanced diet is, of course, an indispensable part of nature cure. 8

The science of natural therapeutics is based on a use, in the treatment of disease, of the same five elements which constitute the human body. 9

Earth

Just lays great emphasis on the use of earth. I felt that I ought to give it a trial. For constipation, Just advises cold mud poultice on the lower abdomen. I made a mud poultice by mixing clean dry earth with water, packed it in a piece of thin cloth and kept it on the abdomen throughout the night. The result was most satisfactory. 10

The mud poultice should be 3 inches broad, 6 inches long and ½ inch thick. 11

It is my experience that a mud poultice applied to the head, relieves headache in most cases. I have tried it in hundreds of cases. Headache may be due to several causes, but whatever the cause, as a general rule, an application of mud poultice relieves it for the time being.

Mud poultices cure ordinary boils. I have applied mud to discharging abscesses as well. For these cases I prepare the poultice by packing the mud in a clean piece of cloth dipped in potassium permanganate lotion, and apply it to the abscess after washing it clean with permanganate lotion. In the majority of cases this treatment results in complete cure. I do not remember a single case in which it has failed me. Mud application immediately relieves the pain of a wasp sting. I have used it in many cases of scorpion bite, though with much less success. 12

In high fever, an application of mud poultice on the head and abdomen is very useful. Although it does not always bring down the temperature, it does invariably soothe the patient and make him feel better so that the patients themselves ask for these applications.

I have used it in several cases of typhoid fever. The fever no doubt runs its own course but mud applications seem to relieve restlessness and abate the suffering. 13

In Sevagram we have made free use of hot mud poultices as a substitute for antiphlogistine. A little oil and salt is added to the mud and it is heated sufficiently long to ensure sterilization. 14

It is safe to use soft alluvial clay, which is neither gritty nor sticky. One should never use earth taken from manured soil. Earth should be dried, pounded, and passed through a fine sieve. If there is any doubt as to its cleanliness, it should be well heated and thus sterilized. 15

Just writes that clean earth may be eaten in order to overcome constipation. Five to ten grams is the maximum dose. The rationale is said to be this. Earth is not digested. It acts as roughage and must pass out. The peirstalsis thus stimulated pushes out the faecal matter as well. I have not tried it myself. Therefore those who wish to do so, should try it on their own responsibility. I am inclined to think that a trial or two is not likely to harm anyone. 16

Water

Hip bath and sitz bath are the most important of Kuhne's contributions to hydro-therapy. He has devised a special tub for use though one can do without it. Any tub thirty to thirty-six inches long according to the patient's height generally serves the purpose. Experience will indicate the proper size. The tub should be filled with fresh cold water so that it does not overflow when the patient sits in it. In summer the water may be iced, if it is not cold enough, to give a gentle shock to the patient. Generally, water kept in earthen jars overnight answers the purpose. Water can also be cooled by putting a piece of cloth on the surface of the water and then fanning it vigorously. The tub should be kept against the bathroom wall and a plank put in the tub to serve as back rest. The patient should sit in the tub keeping his feet outside. Portions of the body outside water should be kept well covered so that the patient does not feel cold. After the patient is comfortably seated in the tub, gentle friction should be applied to his abdomen with a soft towel. This bath can be taken for five to thirty minutes. When it is over, the body should be rubbed dry and the patient put to bed.

Hip bath brings down the temperature in high fever and given in the manner described above it never does any harm, and may do much good. It relieves constipation and improves digestion. The patient feels fresh and active after it. In cases of constipation, Kuhne advises a brisk walk for half an hour immediately after the bath. It should never be given on a full stomach.

I have tried hip baths on a fairly large scale. They have proved efficacious in more than 75 cases out of 100. In cases of hyperpyrexia, if the patient's condition permits of his being seated in the tub, the temperature immediately invariably falls at least by two to three degrees, and the onset of delirium is averted. *17*

Now about the sitz or friction bath. The organ of reproduction is one of the most sensitive parts of the body. There is something illusive about the sensitiveness of the glans penis and the foreskin. Anyway, I know not how to describe it. Kuhne has made use of this knowledge for therapeutic purposes. He advises application of gentle friction to the outer end of the external sexual organ by means of a soft wet piece of cloth, while cold water is being poured. In the case of the male the glans penis should be covered with the foreskin before applying friction. The method advised by Kuhne is this. A stool should be placed in a tub of cold water so that the seat is just about the level of the water in the tub. The patient should sit on the stool with his feet outside the tub and apply gentle friction to the sexual organ which just touches the surface of the water in the tub. This friction should never cause pain. On the contrary the patient should find it pleasant and feel rested and peaceful at the end of the bath. Whatever the ailment, the sitz bath makes the patient feel better for the time being. Kuhne places sitz baths higher than hip baths. I have had much less experience of the former than of the latter. The blame, I think, lies mostly with myself. I have been lax. Those whom I advised sitz baths, have not been patient with the experiment, so that I cannot express an opinion on the efficacy of these baths, based on personal experience. It is worth a trial by everyone. If there is any difficulty about finding a tub, it is possible to pour water from a jug or a *lota* and take the friction bath. It is bound to make the patient feel rested and

peaceful. As a general rule, people pay scant attention to the cleansing of the sexual organ. The friction
bath will easily achieve that end. Unless one is
particularly careful, dirt accumulates between the
foreskin and the glans penis. This must be removed.
Insistence on keeping the sexual organ clean and patiently following the treatment outlined above will make
the observance of Brahmacharya comparatively easier.
It will result in making the local nerve endings less
sensitive and unwanted seminal emissions less likely.
To say the least, it is very unclean to allow seminal
emissions to occur. Greater insistence on cleanliness
should and will cause a feeling of revulsion against
the process and make one much more particular than
otherwise in taking all the precautions to avoid them. 18

Wet sheet packs are also useful in the treatment
of prickly heat, urticaria, other forms of skin irrita-
tion, measles, smallpox etc. I have tried them on a
fairly large scale for these ailments. For smallpox
and measles cases, I added enough potassium permanganate to the water to give it a light pink colour.
The sheet used for these patients, should afterwards
be sterilized by soaking in it boiling water and leaving
it in it till it cools down sufficiently and then washed
with soap and water.

In cases where circulation has become sluggish,
the leg muscles feel sore and there is a peculiar
ache and feelings of discomfort in the legs, an ice
massage does a lot of good. This treatment is more
effective in summer months. Massaging a weak
patient with ice in winter might prove a risky affair.

Now a few words about the therapeutics of hot
water. An intelligent use of hot water gives relief
in many cases. Application of iodine is a very popular

remedy for all sorts of injuries and the like. Application of hot water will prove equally effective in most of these cases. Tincture of iodine is applied on swollen and bruised areas. Hot water fomentations are likely to give equal relief, if not more. Again, iodine drops are used in cases of ear-ache. Irrigation of the ear with warm water is likely to relieve the pain in most of these cases. The use of iodine is attended with certain risks. The patient may have allergy towards the drug. Iodine mistaken for something else and taken internally might prove disastrous. But there is no risk whatsoever in using hot water. Boiling water is as good a disinfectant as tincture of iodine. I do not mean to belittle the usefulness of iodine or suggest that hot water can replace it in all cases. Iodine is one of the few drugs which I regard most useful and necessary, but it is an expensive thing. The poor cannot afford to buy it and moreover its use cannot be safely entrusted to everybody. But water is available everywhere. We may not despise its therapeutic value because it is obtained so easily. Knowledge of common household remedies often proves a godsend in many a crisis. *19*

Steam is a more valuable therapeutic agent. It can be used to make the patient sweat. Steam baths are most useful in cases of rheumatism and other joint-pains. The easiest as well as the oldest method of taking steam bath is this. Spread a blanket or two on a sparsely but tightly woven cot and put one or two covered vessels full with boiling water under it. Make the patient lie flat on the cot and cover him up in such a way that the ends of the covering blankets touch the ground and thus prevent the steam from escaping and the outside air from getting in.

After arranging everything as above, the lid from the vessels containing boiling water is removed and steam soon gets on to the patient lying between the blankets. It may be necessary to change the water once or twice. Usually in India people keep an *angithi* under the pots to keep the water boiling. This ensures continuous discharge of steam, but is attended with risk of accidents. A single spark might set fire to the blankets or to the cot and endanger the patient's life. Therefore, it is advisable to use the method described by me even though it might seem slow and tedious.

Some people add *neem* leaves or other herbs to the water used for generating steam. I do not know if such an addition increases the efficiency of steam. The object is to induce sweat and that is attained by mere steam.

In cases of cold feet or aching of legs, the patient should be made to sit with his feet and legs immersed up to the knees in as hot water as he can bear. A little mustard powder can be added to the water. The foot bath should not last for more than fifteen minutes. This treatment improves the local circulation and gives immediate relief.

In cases of common cold and sore throat a steam kettle which is very much like an ordinary tea kettle with a long nozzle can be used for applying steam to the nose or throat. A rubber tube of required length can be attached to any ordinary kettle for this purpose. [20]

Akash

Akash might be taken for the empty space surrounding the earth and the atmosphere round it. [21]

Sky or the ether is the abode of the atmosphere. One can pump out air say from an empty bottle and create a vacuum, but who can pump out the vacuum itself? That is *akash*.

This *akash* we have to make use of to maintain or to regain health. 22

The more we utilize this great element *akash* the healthier we will be. The first lesson to be learnt is this, that we should not put any partition between ourselves and the sky — the infinite — which is very near and yet very far away. If our bodies could be in contact with the sky without the intervention of houses, roofs and even clothes, we are likely to enjoy the maximum amount of health. This is not possible for everyone. But all can and should accept the validity of the statement and adapt life accordingly. To the extent that we are able to approach the state in practice, we will enjoy contentment and peace of mind. 23

This train of thought will make the thinker keep his surroundings as open as possible. He will not fill the house with unnecessary furniture and will use the minimum of clothes that are necessary. Many households are so packed with all sorts of unnecessary decorations and furniture which one can very well do without, that a simple living man will feel suffocated in those surroundings. They are nothing but means of harbouring dust, bacteria and insects. 24

One should make it a point to sleep in the open. Sufficient covering should be used to protect oneself against the inclemencies of the weather — against cold and dew. In rainy season an umbrella-like roof without walls should be used for keeping the rain out. For

V.S.—13

the rest, the starlit blue canopy should form the roof, so that whenever one opens one's eyes, he or she can feast them on the everchanging beautiful panorama of the heavens. He will never tire of the scene and it will not dazzle or hurt his eyes. On the contrary, it will have a soothing effect on him. To watch the different starry constellations floating in their majesty is a feast for the eyes. One who establishes contact with the stars as living witnesses to all his thoughts will never allow any evil or impurity to enter his mind and will enjoy peaceful, refreshing sleep.

Let us descend from the *akash* above to the *akash* within and immediately about us. Thus the skin has millions of pores. If we fill up the empty space within these pores, we simply die. Any clogging of the pores therefore must interfere with the even flow of health. Similarly we must not fill up the digestive tract with unnecessary foodstuffs. We should eat only as much as we need and no more. Often one overeats or eats indigestible things without being aware of it. An occasional fast, say once a week or once a fortnight, will enable one to keep the balance even. If one is unable to fast for the whole day, one should miss one or more meals during the day. Nature abhors a vacuum is only partially true. Nature constantly demands a vacuum. The vast space surrounding us is the standing testimony of the truth. 25

Sun

Sunbath is as useful as ordinary water bath though the two cannot replace one another. In cases of debility and slow circulation, exposure of the uncovered body to the morning sun acts as an all-round general tonic and accelerates the metabolism. The morning sun has the largest amount of ultra-violet rays which are a most effective component of the sun's rays. If the patient feels cold, he should lie in the sun covered up and gradually expose more and more of his body as he gets used to it. One can also take the sunbath pacing up and down in the sun without any clothes on, in a private enclosure or in any other place away from public gaze. If such a place is not within easy reach, one can just cover up the private parts by tying up a piece of cloth or a *langoti* and expose the rest of his body to the sun. *26*

I know of many persons who have been benefited by sunbaths. It is a well-known treatment for tuberculosis. *27*

Sun treatment often results in the cure of intractable ulcers. *28*

Air

This fifth element is as important as the four already discussed in the foregoing pages. The human body which is composed of the five elements cannot do without any one of them. Therefore no one should be afraid of air. Generally, wherever our people go, they make devices to keep out the sun and the air and thus jeopardize their health. If one cultivates the habit of living in the open in the midst of plenty of fresh air, right from childhood, the body will become hardened and he or she will never suffer from cold in the head and the like ailments. *29*

The Extent of Medical Aid

With the commencement of the activities of the A.I.V.I.A., medical aid finds a prominent, if not almost an exclusive, place on the programme of many workers. The aid consists in distributing among the villagers free medicines, Allopathic, Ayurvedic, Unani or Homeopathic, or all combined. Druggists selling these medicines are quite ready to oblige workers approaching them for a few medicines, which cost them a trifle and which, in their opinion, may, if they look at the gift selfishly, bring them more buyers. The poor patients become the victims of well-intentioned, but ill-informed or over-enthusiastic, workers. More than three-fourths of these drugs are not only useless but imperceptibly, if not perceptibly, harmful to the bodies into which they are put. Where they do bring some temporary relief to the patients, their substitutes are as a rule to be found in the village bazaar.

Therefore, A.I.V.I.A. is leaving medical relief of the kind I have described severely alone. Its primary care is educative in matters of health as well as of economy. Are not both inter-related? Does not health mean wealth for the millions? Their bodies, not their intellect, are the primary instruments of wealth. The Association, therefore, seeks to teach people how to prevent disease. It is well known that the food of the millions is very deficient in its nourishing value. What they do eat they misuse. Their knowledge of hygiene is practically nil. Village sanitation is as bad as it well can be. If, therefore, these defects can be put right and the people imbibe the simple rules of hygiene, most of the ailments they suffer from must disappear without further effort or any outlay of money. Hence the Association does not contemplate opening dispensaries. Investigations are now being made to find out what the villages can supply in the shape of drugs. Satish Babu's cheap remedies* are an effort in that direction. But incredibly simple though they are, he is experimenting with a view to making drastic reduction in the number of these remedies, without diminishing their efficacy. He is studying the bazaar drugs and testing them and comparing them with the corresponding drugs in the British pharmacopoeia. The desire is to wean the simple villagers from the awe of mysterious pills and infusions. 30

Where cases of fever, constipation or such common diseases come to village workers for help they will certainly have to render such help as they can. Where one is certain of the diagnosis, there is no doubt that the village bazaar medicine is the cheapest and best. If one must stock drugs, castor oil, quinine and boiling water are the best medical agents. Castor oil may be locally procurable. The *senna* leaf may serve the same purpose. Quinine I should use sparingly. Every fever does not require quinine treatment. Nor does every fever yield to quinine. Most fevers will disappear after a fast or a semifast. Abstention from cereals, pulses and milk, and taking fruit juices or boiling raisin water, even boiling *gud* water with fresh lemon juice or tamarind, is a semifast. Boiling water is a most powerful medical agent. It may move the bowels, it will induce perspiration and therefore abate fever; it is the safest and cheapest disinfectant. In every case where it is required to be drunk, the water must be allowed to cool till it is fairly bearable to the skin. Boiling does not mean mere heating.

---

* *Home and Village Doctor*, By Satish Chandra Das Gupta, Khadi Pratishthan, 15, College Square, Calcutta.

The water begins to bubble and evaporate after it is on the boil.

Where the workers do not know for certain what to do, they must allow the local *vaidya* to have full sway. Where he is non-existent or unreliable and the workers know a philanthropic doctor nearby, they may invoke his assistance.

But they will find that the most effective way of dealing even with disease is to attend to sanitation. Let them remember that nature is the finest physician. They may be sure that nature is repairing what man has damaged. She appears to have become powerless when man continuously hampers her. Then she sends death — her last and peremptory agent to destroy what is beyond repair — and provides a fresh garment for the wearer. Sanitary and hygienic workers are therefore the best helpers or the best physicians every person has, whether he knows it or not. *31*

Medical relief as part of village work or social service plays an important part in many reports I receive from numerous organizations. This relief consists of medicines supplied to patients who from far and near flock to any person who advertises himself as distributor of such relief. It means no trouble on the part of the medicine man. He need not have much or any knowledge of diseases and the symptoms. Medicines he often receives free from obliging chemists. Donations are always to be had from indiscriminate donors whose conscience is satisfied if they can distribute their charity in aid of suffering humanity.

This social service has appeared to me to be the laziest form of service and often even mischievous. It works mischief when the patient is expected to do nothing save to swallow the drug given to him. He is none the wiser for having received the medicine. If anything he is worse off than before. The knowledge that he can get for nothing or for a trifle, a pill or a potion that will correct certain irregularities will tempt him to repeat them. The fact that he gets such aid free of charge will undermine his self-respect which should disdain to receive anything for nothing.

There is another type of medical relief which is a boon. It is given by those who know the nature of diseases, who will tell the patients why they have their particular complaints and will also tell them how to avoid them. Such servants will rush to assist at all odd hours of the day or night. Such discriminating relief is an education in hygiene, teaching the people how to observe cleanliness and to gain health. But such service is rare. In the majority of cases mention of medical relief in reports is a piece of advertisement leading to donations for other activities requiring perhaps as little exertion or knowledge as medical relief. I would therefore urge all workers in the social field, whether urban or rural, to treat their medical activity as the least important item of service. It would be better to avoid all mention of such relief. Workers would do well to adopt measures that would prevent disease in their localities. Their stock of medicines should be as small as possible. They should study the bazaar medicines available in their villages, know their reputed properties, and use them as far as possible. They will find as we are finding in Sindi (a village near Wardha) that hot water, sunshine, clean salt and soda with an occasional use of castor oil or quinine answer most purposes.

We make it a point to send all serious cases to the
Civil Hospital. Patients flock to Mirabahen and
receive lessons in hygiene and prevention of diseases.
They do not resent this method of approach instead
of simply being given a powder or a mixture. *32*

CHAPTER 25

DIET

Whilst it is true that man cannot live without air
and water, the thing that nourishes the body is food.
Hence the saying, food is life.

Food can be divided into three categories :
vegetarian, flesh and mixed. Flesh foods include
fowl and fish. Milk is an animal product and cannot
by any means be included in a strictly vegetarian
diet. It serves the purpose of meat to a very large
extent. In medical language it is classified as animal
food. A layman does not consider milk to be animal
food. On the other hand, eggs are regarded by the
layman as a flesh food. In reality, they are not.
Nowadays sterile eggs are also produced. The hen
is not allowed to see the cock and yet it lays eggs.
A sterile egg never develops into a chick. Therefore,
he who can take milk should have no objection to
taking sterile eggs.

Medical opinion is mostly in favour of a mixed
diet, although there is a growing school, which is
strongly of the opinion that anatomical and physiologi-
cal evidence is in favour of man being a vegetarian.
His teeth, his stomach, intestines etc. seem to prove
that nature has meant man to be a vegetarian.

Vegetarian diet, besides grains, pulses, edible roots, tubers and leaves, includes fruits, both fresh and dry. Dry fruit includes nuts like almonds, pistachio, walnut etc.

I have always been in favour of pure vegetarian diet. But experience has taught me that in order to keep perfectly fit, vegetarian diet must include milk and milk products such as curds, butter, *ghee* etc. This is a significant departure from my original idea. I excluded milk from my diet for six years. At that time, I felt none the worse for the denial. But in the year 1917, as a result of my own ignorance, I was laid on with severe dysentery. I was reduced to a skeleton, but I stubbornly refused to take any medicine and with equal stubborness refused to take milk or buttermilk. But I could not build up my body and pick up sufficient strength to leave the bed. I had taken a vow of not taking milk. A medical friend suggested that at the time of taking the vow, I could have had in mind only the milk of the cow and buffalo; why should the vow prevent me from taking goat's milk? My wife supported him and I yielded. Really speaking, for one who has given up milk, though at the time of taking the vow only the cow and the buffalo were in mind, milk should be taboo. All animal milks have practically the same composition, though the proportion of the components varies in each case. So I may be said to have kept merely the letter, not the spirit, of the vow. Be that as it may, goat's milk was produced immediately and I drank it. It seemed to bring me new life. I picked up rapidly and was soon able to leave the bed. On account of this and several similar experiences, I have been forced to admit the necessity of adding milk to the strict vegetarian diet. But I am convinced that in the vast vegetable kingdom there must be some kind, which, while supplying those necessary substances which we derive from milk and meat, is free from their drawbacks, ethical and other.

In my opinion there are definite drawbacks in taking milk or meat. In order to get meat we have to kill. And we are certainly not entitled to any other milk except the mother's milk in our infancy. Over and above the moral drawback, there are others, purely from the point of view of health. Both milk and meat bring with them the defects of the animal from which they are derived. Domesticated cattle are hardly ever perfectly healthy. Just like man, cattle suffer from innumerable diseases. Several of these are overlooked even when the cattle are subjected to periodical medical examinations. Besides, medical examination of all the cattle in India seems to be an impossible feat, at any rate for the present. I am conducting a dairy at the Sevagram Ashram. I can easily get help from medical friends. Yet I cannot say with certainty that all the cattle in the Sevagram Dairy are healthy. On the contrary, a cow that had been considered to be healthy by everybody was found to be suffering from tuberculosis. Before this diagnosis was made, the milk of that cow had been used regularly in the Ashram. The Ashram also takes milk from the farmers in the neighbourhood. Their cattle have not been medically examined. It is difficult to determine whether a particular specimen of milk is safe for consumption or not. We have to rest content with as much safety as boiling of the milk can assure us of. If the Ashram cannot boast of foolproof medical examination of its cattle, and be certain of the safety of its dairy products, the situation elsewhere is not likely to be much better. What applies to the milch cattle applies to a much greater extent to the animals slaughtered for meat. As a general rule, man just depends upon luck to escape from such risks. He does not seem to worry much about his health. He considers himself to be quite safe in his medical fortress in the shape of doctors, *vaids* and *hakims*. His main worry and concern is how to get wealth and position in society. This worry overshadows all the rest. Therefore, so long as some selfless scientist does not, as a result of patient research work, discover a vegetable substitute for milk and meat, man will go on taking meat and milk.

Now let us consider mixed diet. Man requires food which can supply tissue building substances to provide for the growth and daily wear and tear of the body. It should also contain something which can supply energy, fat, certain salts and roughage to help the excretion of waste matter. Tissue building substances are known as proteins. They are obtained from milk, meat, eggs, pulses and nuts. The proteins contained in milk and meat, in other words, the animal proteins being more easily digestible and assimilable, are much more valuable than vegetable proteins. Milk is superior to meat. The medicoes tell us that in cases where meat cannot be digested, milk is digested quite easily. For vegetarians milk being the only source of animal proteins, is a very important article of diet. The proteins in raw eggs are considered to be the most easily digestible of all proteins.

But everybody cannot afford to drink milk. And milk is not available in every place. I would like to mention here a very important fact with regard to milk. Contrary to the popular belief, skimmed milk is a very valuable article of diet. There are times when it proves even more useful than whole milk. The chief function of milk is to supply animal proteins for tissue building and tissue repair. Skimming, while it partially removes the fats, does not affect the proteins at all. Moreover, the available skimming instruments cannot remove all the fat from milk. Neither is there any likelihood of such an instrument being constructed.

The body requires other things besides milk, whole or skimmed. I give the second place to cereals — wheat, rice, *juwar*, *bajri* etc. These are used as the staple diet. Different cereals are used as staple in different provinces of India. In many places, more than one kind of cereals are eaten at the same time for instance, small quantities of wheat, *bajri* and rice are often served together. This mixture is not necessary for the nourishment of the body. It makes it difficult to regulate the quantity of food intake, and puts an extra strain upon digestion. As all these varieties supply starch mainly, it is better to take one only, at a time. Wheat may well be described as the king among the cereals. If we glance at the world map, we find that wheat occupies the first place. From the point of view of health, if we can get wheat, rice and other cereals become unnecessary. If wheat is not available and *juwar* etc. cannot be taken on account of dislike or difficulty in digesting them, rice has to be resorted to.

The cereals should be properly cleansed, ground on a grinding stone, and the resulting flour used as it is. Sieving of the flour should be avoided. It is likely to remove the *bhusi* or the pericarp which is a rich source of salts and vitamins, both of which are most valuable from the point of view of nutrition. The pericarp also supplies roughage, which helps the action of the bowels. Rice grain being very delicate, nature has provided it with an outer covering or epicarp. This is not edible. In order to remove this inedible portion, rice has to be pounded. Pounding should be just sufficient to remove the epicarp on the outer skin of the rice grain. But machine pounding not only removes the outer skin, but also polishes the rice by removing its pericarp. The explanation of the popularity of polished rice lies in the fact that polishing helps preservation. The pericarp is very sweet and unless it is removed, rice is easily attacked by certain organisms. Polished rice and wheat without its pericarp, supply us with almost pure starch. Important constituents of the cereals are lost with the removal of the pericarp. The pericarp of rice is sold as rice polishings. This and the pericarp of wheat can be cooked and eaten by themselves. They can be also made into *chapatis* or cakes. It is possible that rice *chapatis* may be more easily digestible than whole rice and in this form a lesser quantity may result in full satisfaction.

We are in the habit of dipping each morsel of the *chapati* in vegetable or *dal* gravy before eating it. The result is that most people swallow their food without proper mastication. Mastication is an important step in the process of digestion, especially that of starch. Digestion of starch begins on its coming into contact with saliva in the mouth. Mastication ensures a thorough mixing of food with saliva. Therefore, starchy foods should be eaten in a relatively dry form, which results in a greater flow of saliva and also necessitates their thorough mastication.

After the starch supplying cereals come the protein supplying pulses—beans, lentils etc. Almost everybody seems to think that pulses are an essential constituent of diet. Even meat eaters must have pulses. It is easy to understand that those who have to do hard manual work and who cannot afford to drink milk, cannot do without pulses. But I can say without any hesitation whatsoever that those who follow sedentary occupations as for instance, clerks, businessmen, lawyers, doctors, teachers and those who are not too poor to buy milk, do not require pulses. Pulses are generally considered to be difficult to digest and are eaten in a much smaller quantity than cereals. Out of the varieties of pulses, peas, gram and haricot beans are considered to be the most and *mung* and *masoor* (lentils) the least difficult to digest.

Vegetables and fruits should come third on our list. One would expect them to be cheap and easily available in India. But it is not so. They are generally considered to be delicacies meant for the city people. In the villages fresh vegetables are a rarity, and in most places fruit is also not available. This shortage of greens and fruits is a slur on the administration of India. The villagers can grow plenty of green vegetables if they wish to. The question of fruit cannot be solved so easily. The land legislation is bad from the villager's standpoint. But I am transgressing.

Among fresh vegetables, a fair amount of leafy vegetables must be taken every day. I do not include potatoes, sweet potatoes, *suran* etc., which supply starch mainly, among vegetables. They should be put down in the same category as starch supplying cereals. A fair helping of ordinary fresh vegetables is advisable. Certain varieties such as cucumber, tomatoes, mustard and cress and other tender leaves need not be cooked. They should be washed properly and then eaten raw in small quantities.

As for fruits, our daily diet should include the available fruits of the season, e.g. mangoes, *jambu*, guavas, grapes, *papaiyas*, limes—sweet or sour, oranges, *moosambi*, etc. should all be used in their season. The best time for taking fruit is in the early morning. A breakfast of fruit and milk should give full satisfaction. Those who take an early lunch may well have a breakfast of fruit only.

Banana is a good fruit. But as it is very rich in starch, it takes the place of bread. Milk and banana make a perfect meal.

A certain amount of fat is also necessary. This can be had in the form of *ghee* or oil. If *ghee* can be had, oil becomes unnecessary. It is difficult to digest and is not so nourishing as pure *ghee*. An ounce and a half of *ghee* per head per day, should be considered ample to supply the needs of the body. Whole milk also is a source of *ghee*. Those who cannot afford it should take enough oil to supply the need for fat. Among oils, sweet oil, groundnut oil and cocoa-nut oil should be given preference. Oil must be fresh. If available, it is better to use hand-pressed oil. Oil and *ghee* sold in the bazaar are generally quite useless. It is a matter of great sorrow and shame. But so long as honesty has not become an integral part of business morals, whether through legislation or through education, the individual will have to procure the pure article with patience and diligence. One should never be satisfied to take what one can get, irrespective of its quality. It is far better to do without *ghee* and oil altogether than to eat rancid oil and adulterated *ghee*. As in the case of fats, a certain amount of sugar is also necessary. Although sweet fruits supply plenty of sugar, there is no harm in taking one to one and a half ounces of sugar, brown or white, in the day. If one cannot get sweet fruits, sugar may become a necessity. But the undue prominence given to sweet things nowadays is wrong. City folk eat too much of sweet things. Milk puddings, milk sweets and sweets of other kinds are consumed in large quantities. They are all unnecessary and are harmful except when taken in very small quantities. It may be said without any fear of exaggeration that to partake of sweetmeats and other delicacies, in a country where the millions do not even get an ordinary full meal, is equivalent to robbery.

What applies to sweets, applies with equal force to *ghee* and oil. There is no need to eat food fried in *ghee* or oil. To use up *ghee* in making *puris* and *laddus* is thoughtless extravagance. Those who are not used to such food cannot eat these things at all. For instance, Englishmen on their first coming into our country cannot eat our sweets and fried foodstuffs. Those that do eat them I have often seen fall ill. Taste is acquired, not born with us. All the delicacies of the world cannot equal the relish that hunger gives to food. A hungry man will eat a dry piece of bread with the greatest relish, whereas one who is not hungry will refuse the best of sweetmeats.

Now let us consider how often and how much should one eat. Food should be taken as a matter of duty—even as a medicine—to sustain the body, never for the satisfaction of the palate. Thus, pleasurable feeling comes from satisfaction of real hunger. Therefore, we can say that relish is dependent upon hunger and not outside it. Because of our wrong habits and artificial way of living, very few people know what their system requires. Our parents who bring us into this world do not, as a rule, cultivate self-control. Their habits and their way of living influence the children to a certain extent. The mother's food during pregnancy is bound to affect the child. After that during childhood, the mother pampers the child with all sorts of tasty foods. She gives the child a little bit out of whatever she herself may be eating and the child's digestive system gets a wrong training from its infancy. Habits once formed are difficult to shed. There are very few who succeed in getting rid of them. But when the realization comes to man that he is his own bodyguard, and his body has been dedicated to service, he desires to learn the laws of keeping his body in a fit condition and tries hard to follow them.

We have now reached a point when we can lay down the amount of various foods required by a man of sedentary habits, which most men and women who will read these pages, are.

Cow's milk	2 lbs.
Cereals (wheat, rice, *bajri*, in all)	6 oz.
Vegetables leafy	3 oz.
,, others	5 oz.
,, raw	1 oz.
Ghee	1½ oz.
or Butter	2 oz.
Gur or white sugar	1½ oz.

V.S.-14

Fresh fruit according to one's taste and purse. In any case it is good to take two sour limes a day. The juice should be squeezed and taken with vegetables or in water, cold or hot.

All these weights are of raw stuff. I have not put down the amount of salt. It should be added afterwards according to taste.

Now, how often should one eat? Many people take two meals a day. The general rule is to take three meals: breakfast early in the morning and before going out to work, dinner at midday and supper in the evening or later. There is no necessity to have more than three meals. In the cities some people keep on nibbling from time to time. This habit is harmful. The digestive apparatus requires rest. *1*

CHAPTER 26

VILLAGE PROTECTION

Peace Brigade

Some time ago I suggested the formation of a Peace Brigade whose members would risk their lives in dealing with riots, especially communal. The idea was that this Brigade should substitute the police and even the military. This reads ambitious. The achievement may prove impossible. Yet, if the Congress is to succeed in its non-violent struggle, it must develop the power to deal peacefully with such situations.

Let us therefore see what qualifications a member of the contemplated Peace Brigade should possess.

(1) He or she must have a living faith in non-violence. This is impossible without a living faith in God. A non-violent man can do nothing save by the power and grace of God. Without it he won't have the courage to die without anger, without fear and without retaliation. Such courage comes from the belief that God sits in the hearts of all and that there should be no fear in the presence of God. The knowledge of the omnipresence of God also means respect for the lives of even those who may be called opponents or goondas. This contemplated intervention is a process of stilling the fury of man when the brute in him gets the mastery over him.

(2) This messenger of peace must have equal regard for all the principal religions of the earth. Thus, if he is a Hindu, he will respect the other faiths current in India. He must therefore possess a knowledge of the general principles of the different faiths professed in the country.

(3) Generally speaking, this work of peace can only be done by local men in their own localities.

(4) The work can be done singly or in groups. Therefore no one need wait for companions. Nevertheless one would naturally seek companions in one's own locality and form a local Brigade.

(5) This messenger of peace will cultivate through personal service contacts with the people in his locality or chosen circle, so that when he appears to deal with ugly situations, he does not descend upon the members of a riotous assembly as an utter stranger liable to be looked upon as a suspect or an unwelcome visitor.

(6) Needless to say, a peace bringer must have a character beyond reproach and must be known for his strict impartiality.

(7) Generally there are previous warnings of coming storms. If these are known, the Peace Brigade will not wait till the conflagration breaks out but will try to handle the situation in anticipation.

(8) Whilst, if the movement spreads, it might be well if there are some whole-time workers, it is not absolutely necessary that there should be. The idea is to have as many good and true men and women as possible. These can be had only if volunteers are drawn from those who are engaged in various walks of life but have leisure enough to cultivate friendly relations with the people living in their ·circle and otherwise possess the qualifications required of a member of the Peace Brigade.

(9) There should be a distinctive dress worn by the members of the contemplated Brigade so that in course of time they will be recognized without the slightest difficulty.

These are but general suggestions. Each centre can work out its own constitution on the basis here suggested. *1*

My Idea of a Police Force

Even in a non-violent State a police force may be necessary. This, I admit, is a sign of my imperfect Ahimsa. I have not the courage to declare that we can carry on without a police force as I have in respect of an army. Of course I can and do envisage a state where the police will not be necessary; but whether we shall succeed in realizing it, the future alone will show.

The police of my conception will, however, be of a wholly different pattern from the present-day force. Its ranks will be composed of believers in non-violence.

They will be servants, not masters, of the people. The people will instinctively render them every help, and through mutual co-operation they will easily deal with the ever-decreasing disturbances. The police force will have some kind of arms, but they will be rarely used, if at all. In fact the policemen will be reformers. Their police work will be confined primarily to robbers and dacoits. Quarrels between labour and capital and strikes will be few and far between in a non-violent State, because the influence of the non-violent majority will be so great as to command the respect of the principal elements in society. Similarly there will be no room for communal disturbances. 2

Non-violent Volunteer Corps

Some time ago an attempt was made, at my instance, to form *shanti dals* but nothing came of it. This lesson, however, was learnt that the membership, in its very nature, of such organizations could not be large. Ordinarily, the efficient running of a large volunteer corps based on force implies the possibility of the use of force in the event of breach of discipline. In such bodies little or no stress is laid on a man's character. Physique is the chief factor. The contrary must obtain in non-violent bodies in which character or soul force must mean everything and physique must take second place. It is difficult to find many such persons. That is why non-violent corps must be small, if they are to be efficient. Such Brigades may be scattered all over; there may be one each for a village or a *mohalla*. The members must know one another well. Each corps will select its own head. All the members will have the same status, but where everyone is doing the same work there must be one person under whose discipline all must come, or else the work will suffer. Where there are two or more Brigades the leaders must consult among themselves and decide on a common line of action. In that way alone lies success.

If non-violent volunteer corps are formed on the above lines, they çan easily stop trouble. These corps will not require all the physical training given in *akhadas*, but a certain part of it will be necessary.

One thing, however, should be common to members of all such organizations and that is implicit faith in God. He is the only companion and doer. Without faith in Him these Peace Brigades will be lifeless. By whatever name one calls God, one must realize that one can only work through His strength. Such a man will never take another's life. He will allow himself, if need be, to be killed and thereby live through his victory over death.

The mind of the man in whose life the realization of this law has become a living reality will not be bewildered in crisis. He will instinctively know the right way to act.

In spite, however, of what I have said above, I would like to give some rules culled from my own experience :

1. A volunteer may not carry any weapons.

2. The members of a corps must be easily recognizable.

3. Every volunteer must carry bandages, scissors, needle and thread, surgical knife, etc. for rendering first aid.

4. He should know how to carry and remove the wounded.

5. He should know how to put out fires, how to enter a fire area without getting burnt, how to climb heights for rescue work and descend safely with or without his charge.

6. He should be well acquainted with all the residents of his locality. This is a service in itself.

7. He should recite *Ramanama* ceaselessly in his heart and persuade others who believe to do likewise.

Man often repeats the name of God parrot-wise and expects fruit from so doing. The true seeker must have that living faith which will not only dispel the untruth of parrot-wise repetition from within him but also from the hearts of others. 3

CHAPTER 27

THE VILLAGE WORKER

The Ideal Village Worker

I propose to speak to you about the ideal of work and life that you have to keep in view and work towards.

You are here not for a career in the current sense of the term. Today man's worth is measured in Rs. as. ps. and a man's educational training is an article of commerce. If you have come with that measure in mind, you are doomed to disappointment. At the end of your studies you may start with an honorarium of ten rupees and end with it. You may not compare it with what a manager of a great firm or a high official gets.

We have to change the current standards. We promise you no earthly careers, in fact we want to wean you from ambition of that kind. You are expected to keep your food-bill within Rs 6 a month. The food-bill of an I.C.S. may come to Rs 60 a month, but that does not mean that he is or will be on that account physically or intellectually or morally superior to you. He may be for all his sumptuous living even inferior in all these respects. You have come to this institution because, I presume, you do not value your qualifications in metal. You delight in giving your service to the country for a mere pittance. A man may earn thousands of rupees on the Stock Exchange but may be thoroughly useless for our purposes. They would be unhappy in our humble surroundings and we should be unhappy in theirs. We want ideal labourers in the country's cause. They will not bother about what food they get, or what comforts they are assured by the villagers whom they serve. They will trust to God for whatever they need, and will exult in the trials and tribulations they might have to undergo. This is inevitable in our country where we have 7,00,000 villages to think of. We cannot afford to have a salaried staff of workers who have an eye to regular increments, provident funds and pensions. Faithful service of the villagers is its own satisfaction.

Some of you will be tempted to ask if this is also the standard for the villagers. Not by any means. These prospects are for us servants and not for the village folk our masters. We have sat on their backs all these years, and we want to accept voluntary and increasing poverty in order that our masters' lot may be much better than it is today. We have to enable them to earn much more than they are earning today. That is the aim of the Village Industries Association. It cannot prosper unless it has an ever-increasing number of servants such as I have described. May you be such servants. *1*

Requisite Qualifications

[The following are some qualifications prescribed by Gandhiji for Satyagrahis. But as a village worker was according to him also to be a true Satyagrahi, these qualifications may be regarded as applying also to a village worker. —Ed.]

1. He must have a living faith in God, for He is his only Rock.

2. He must believe in truth and non-violence as his creed and therefore have faith in the inherent goodness of human nature which he expects to evoke by his truth and love expressed through his suffering.

3. He must be leading a chaste life and be ready and willing for the sake of his cause to give up his life and his possessions.

4. He must be a habitual Khadi-wearer and spinner. This is essential for India.

5. He must be a teetotaller and be free from the use of other intoxicants in order that his reason may be always unclouded and his mind constant.

6. He must carry out with a willing heart all the rules of discipline as may be laid down from time to time.

The qualifications are not to be regarded as exhaustive. They are illustrative only. *2*

His Duties

1. Every worker shall be a habitual wearer of Khadi made from self-spun yarn or certified by the A. I. S. A. and must be a teetotaller. If a Hindu, he must have abjured untouchability in any shape or form in his own person or in his family and must be a believer in the ideal of inter-communal unity, equal respect and regard for all religions and equality of opportunity and status for all irrespective of race, creed or sex.

2. He shall come in personal contact with every villager within his jurisdiction.

3. He shall enrol and train workers from amongst the villagers and keep a register of all these.

4. He shall keep a record of his work from day to day.

5. He shall organize the villages so as to make them self-contained and self-supporting through their agriculture and handicrafts.

6. He shall educate the village folk in sanitation and hygiene and take all measures for prevention of ill health and disease among them.

7. He shall organize the education of the village folk from birth to death along the lines of *Nayee Talim*, in accordance with the policy laid down by the Hindustani Talimi Sangh.

8. He shall see that those whose names are missing on the statutory voters' roll are duly entered therein.

9. He shall encourage those who have not yet acquired the legal qualification, to acquire it for getting the right of franchise. 3

Village Work

The centre of the village worker's life will be the spinning wheel. The idea at the back of Khadi is that it is an industry supplementary to agriculture and co-extensive with it. The spinning wheel cannot be said to have been established in its own proper place in our life, until we can banish idleness from our villages and make every village home a busy hive.

The worker will not only be spinning regularly but will be working for his bread with the adze or the spade or the last, as the case may be. All his hours minus the eight hours of sleep and rest will be fully occupied with some work. He will have no time to waste. He will allow himself no laziness and allow others none. His life will be a constant lesson to his neighbours in ceaseless and joy-giving industry. Our compulsory or voluntary idleness has to go. If it does not go, no panacea will be of any avail, and semi-starvation will remain the eternal problem that it is. He who eats two grains must produce four. Unless the law is accepted as universal, no amount of reduction in population would serve to solve the problem. If the law is accepted and observed, we have room enough to accommodate millions more to come.

The village worker will thus be a living embodiment of industry. He will master all the processes of Khadi, from cotton-sowing and picking to weaving, and will devote all his thought to perfecting them. If he treats it as a science, it won't jar on him, but he will derive fresh joy from it everyday, as he realizes more and more its great possibilities. If he will go to the village as a teacher, he will go there no less as a learner. He will soon find that he has much to learn from the simple villagers. He will enter into every

detail of village life, he will discover the village handicrafts and investigate the possibilities of their growth
and their improvement. He may find the villagers
completely apathetic to the message of Khadi, but he
will, by his life of service, compel interest and attention. Of course, he will not forget his limitations and
will not engage in, for him, the futile task of solving
the problem of agricultural indebtedness.

Sanitation and hygiene will engage a good part
of his attention. His home and his surroundings will
not only be a model of cleanliness, but he will help
to promote sanitation in the whole village by taking
the broom and the basket round.

He will not attempt to set up a village dispensary
or to become the village doctor. These are traps which
must be avoided. I happened during my Harijan tour
to come across a village where one of our workers
who should have known better had built a pretentious
building in which he had housed a dispensary and
was distributing free medicine to the villages around.
In fact, the medicines were being taken from home to
home by volunteers and the dispensary was described
as boasting a register of 1,200 patients a month! I
had naturally to criticize this severely. That was not
the way to do village work, I told him. His duty was
to inculcate lessons of hygiene and sanitation in the
village folk and thus to show them the way of
preventing illness, rather than attempt to cure them. I
asked him to leave the palace-like building and to
hire it out to the Local Board and to settle in thatched
huts. All that one need stock in the way of drugs is
quinine, castor oil and iodine and the like. The worker should concentrate more on helping people realize

the value of personal and village cleanliness and maintaining it at all cost.

Then he will interest himself in the welfare of the village Harijans. His home will be open to them. In fact, they will turn to him naturally for help in their troubles and difficulties. If the village folk will not suffer him to have the Harijan friends in his house situated in their midst, he must take up his residence in the Harijan quarters.

A word about the knowledge of the alphabet. It has its place, but I should warn you against a misplaced emphasis on it. Do not proceed on the assumption that you cannot proceed with rural instruction without first teaching the children or adults how to read and write. Lots of useful information on current affairs, history, geography and elementary arithmetic, can be given by word of mouth before the alphabet is touched. The eyes, the ears and the tongue come before the hand. Reading comes before writing, and drawing before tracing the letters of the alphabet. If this natural method is followed, the understanding of the children will have a much better opportunity of development than when it is under check by beginning the children's training with the alphabet.

The worker's life will be in tune with the village life. He will not pose as a litterateur buried in his books, loathe to listen to details of humdrum life. On the contrary, the people, whenever they see him, will find him busy with his tools—spinning wheel, loom, adze, spade, etc.—and always responsive to their meanest inquiries. He will always insist on working for his bread. God has given to everyone the capacity of producing more than his daily needs and, if he will only use his resourcefulness, he will not be in want of an occupation suited to his capacities, however poor they may be. It is more likely than not that the people will gladly maintain him, but it is not improbable that in some places he may be given a cold shoulder. He will still plod on. It is likely that in some villages he may be boycotted for his pro-Harijan proclivities. Let him in that case approach the Harijans and·look to them to provide him with food. The labourer is always worthy of his hire and, if he conscientiously serves them, let him not hesitate to accept his food from the Harijans, always provided that he gives more than he takes. In the very early stages, of course, he will draw his meagre allowance from a central fund where such is possible.

Remember that our weapons are spiritual. It is a force that works irresistibly, if imperceptibly. Its progress is geometrical rather than arithmetical. It never ceases so long as there is a propeller behind. The background of all your activities has, therefore, to be spiritual. Hence the necessity for the strictest purity of conduct and character.

You will not tell me that this is an impossible programme, that you have not the qualifications for it. That you have not fulfilled it so far should be no impediment in your way. If it appeals to your reason and your heart, you must not hesitate. Do not fight shy of the experiment. The experiment will itself provide the momentum for more and more effort. 4

Items of Village Work

The very first problem the village worker will solve is its sanitation. It is the most neglected

of all the problems that baffle workers and that undermine physical well-being and breed disease. If the
worker became a voluntary *bhangi*, he would begin
by collecting night-soil and turn it into manure and
sweeping village streets. He will tell people how and
where they should perform daily functions and speak
to them on the value of sanitation and the great
injury caused by its neglect. The worker will continue
to do the work whether the villagers listen to him or
no. 5

If rural reconstruction were not to include rural
sanitation, our villages would remain the muck-heap
that they are today. Village sanitation is a vital part
of village life and is as difficult as it is important. It
needs a heroic effort to eradicate age-long insanitation. The village worker who is ignorant of the
science of village sanitation, who is not a successful
scavenger, cannot fit himself for village service.

It seems to be generally admitted that without the
new or basic education the education of millions of
children in India is well-nigh impossible. The village
worker has, therefore, to master it, and become a
basic education teacher himself.

Adult education will follow in the wake of basic
education as a matter of course. Where this new
education has taken root, the children themselves
become their parents' teachers. Be that as it may,
the village worker has to undertake adult education
also.

Woman is described as man's better half. As
long as she has not the same rights in law as man, as
long as the birth of a girl does not receive the same
welcome as that of a boy, so long we should know that
India is suffering from partial paralysis. Suppression

of woman is a denial of Ahimsa. Every village
worker will, therefore, regard every woman as his
mother, sister or daughter as the case may be, and
look upon her with respect. Only such a worker
will command the confidence of the village people.

It is impossible for an unhealthy people to win
Swaraj. Therefore we should no longer be guilty of
the neglect of the health of our people. Every village
worker must have a knowledge of the general principles of health.

Without a common language no nation can come
into being. Instead of worrying himself with the controversy about Hindi-Hindustani and Urdu, the village worker will acquire a knowledge of the *rashtra-
bhasha*, which should be such as can be understood
by both Hindus and Muslims.

Our infatuation for English has made us unfaith-
ful to provincial languages. If only as penance for
this unfaithfulness the village worker should cultivate
in the villagers a love of their own speech. He will
have equal regard for all the other languages of India,
and will learn the language of the part where he may
be working, and thus be able to inspire the villagers
there with a regard for their own speech.

The whole of this programme will, however, be
a structure on sand if it is not built on the solid foundation of economic equality. Economic equality must
never be supposed to mean possession of an equal
amount of worldy goods by everyone. It does mean,
however, that everyone will have a proper house to
live in, sufficient and balanced food to eat, and sufficient Khadi with which to cover himself. It also
means that the cruel inequality that obtains today
will be removed by purely non-violent means. 6

A Talk to Village Workers

Khadi will certainly occupy the centre of the village industries. But remember that we have to concentrate on making the villages self-sufficing in Khadi. Out of self-sufficing Khadi will follow commercial Khadi as a matter of course.

You will of course take up any other industry available in villages and for which you can find a market, care being taken that no shop has to be run at a loss and no article produced for which there is no market. Give eight hours of your day to any home craft you like and show to the villagers that as you earn your wage, even so can they earn it by eight hours' work.

You will also not take a companion to work with you. Our policy is to send a single worker to a village or group of villages. That will enable him to bring his resourcefulness into full play. He may pick out any number of companions from the village itself. They will work under his direction, but he will be mainly responsible for the village under his charge.

Let us not be tempted by the allurements of the machine age; let us concentrate on rendering our own body-machines perfect and efficient instruments of work, and let us get the best out of them. This is your task. Go ahead with it, without flinching. 7

Fear Complex

Many workers are so frightened of village life that they fear that if they are not paid by some agency they will not be able to earn their living by labouring in villages, especially if they are married and have a family to support. In my opinion this is a demoralizing belief. No doubt, if a person goes to a village with a city mentality and wants to live in villages the city life, he will never earn enough unless he, like the city people, exploits the villagers. But if a person settles in a village and tries to live like the villagers, he should have no difficulty in making a living by the sweat of his brow. He should have confidence that if the villagers who are prepared to toil all the year round in the traditional unintelligent manner can earn their living, he must also earn at least as much as the average villager. This he will do without displacing a single villager, for he will go to a village as a producer, not as a parasite.

If the worker has the ordinary size family, his wife and one other member should be full-time workers. Such a worker won't immediately have the muscle of the villager, but he will more than make up for the deficiency by his intelligence, if only he will shed his diffidence and fear complex. He would be doing productive work, and not be a mere consumer, unless he gets an adequate response from the villagers, so as to occupy the whole of his time in serving them. In that case he will be worth the commission on the additional production of the villagers induced by his effort. But the experience of the few months that the village work has gone on under the aegis of the A.I.V.I.A. shows that the response from the villagers will be very slow and that the worker will have to become a pattern of virtue and work before the villagers. That will be the best object-lesson for them which is bound to impress them sooner or later, provided that he lives as one of them and not as a patron seated amongst them to be adored from a respectful distance.

The question, therefore, is what remunerative work can he do in the village of his choice? He and the members of the family will give some time to cleaning the village, whether the villagers help him or not, and he will give them such simple medical assistance as is within his power to give. Every person can prescribe a simple opening drug or quinine, wash a boil or wound, wash dirty eyes and ears, and apply a clean ointment to a wound. I am trying to find out a book that will give the simplest directions in the ordinary cases occurring daily in the villages. Anyway these two things must be an integral part of village work. They ought not to occupy more than two hours of his time per day. The village worker has no such thing as an eight hours' day. For him the labour for the villager is a labour of love. For his living, therefore, he will give eight hours at least in addition to the two hours. It should be borne in mind that under the new scheme propounded by the A.I.S.A. and A.I.V.I.A. all labour has an equal minimum value. Thus a carder who works at his bow for one hour and turns out the average quantity of cards will get exactly the same wage that the weaver, the spinner or the paper-maker would, for the given quantity of their respective work per hour. Therefore, the worker is free to choose and learn whatever work he can easily do, care being always taken to choose such labour whose product is easily saleable in his village or the surrounding area or is in demand by the Associations.

One great need in every village is an honest shop where unadulterated food-stuffs and other things can be had for the cost price and a moderate commission. It is true that a shop, be it ever so small, requires some capital. But a worker who is at all known in the area of his work should command sufficient confidence in his honesty to enable him to make small wholesale purchases on credit.

I may not take these concrete suggestions much further. An observant worker will always make important discoveries and soon know what labour he can do to earn a living and be at the same time an object-lesson to the villagers whom he is to serve. He will therefore have to choose labour that will not exploit the villagers, that will not injure their health or morals but will teach the villagers to take up industries to occupy their leisure hours and add to their tiny incomes. His observations will lead him to direct his attention to the village wastes including weeds and the superficial natural resources of the village. He will soon find that he can turn many of them to good account. If he picks up edible weeds, it is as good as earning part of his food. Mirabehn has presented me with a museum of beautiful marble-like stones which serve several useful purposes as they are, and I would soon convert them into bazaar articles if I had leisure and would invest into simple tools to give them different shapes. Kakasaheb had, given to him, split bamboo waste that was destined to be burnt, and with a rude knife he turned some of it into paper knives and wooden spoons both saleable in limited quantities. Some workers in Maganwadi occupy their leisure in making envelopes out of waste paper blank on one side.

The fact is the villagers have lost all hope. They suspect that every stranger's hand is at their throats and that he goes to them only to exploit them. Divorce between intellect and labour has paralysed their thinking faculty. Their working hours they do not use to the best advantage. The worker should enter such villages full of love and hope, feeling sure that where men and women labour unintelligently and remain unemployed half the year round, he, working all the year round and combining labour with intelligence, cannot fail to win the confidence of the villagers and earn his living honestly and well by labouring in their midst.

'But what about my children and their education?' says the candidate worker. If the children are to receive their education after the modern style, I can give no useful guidance. If it be deemed enough to make them healthy, sinewy, honest, intelligent villagers, any day able to earn their livelihood in the home of their parents' adoption, they will have their all-round education under the parental roof and withal they will be partly earning members of the family from the moment they reach the years of understanding and are able to use their hands and feet in a methodical manner. There is no school equal to a decent home and no teachers equal to honest virtuous parents. Modern high school education is a dead weight on the villagers. Their children will never be able to get it, and thank God they will never miss it if they have the training of the decent home. If the village worker is not a decent man or woman, capable of conducting a decent home, he or she had better not aspire after the high privilege and honour of becoming a village worker. *8*

Village Workers' Questions

I

[At the workers' meeting instead of asking Gandhiji to address them they gave him a list of questions on which he was requested to enlighten them. Questions were about the duties of the village workers, their livelihood, body labour, maintaining a diary, working among *dublas* of Gujarat etc.]

The only duty of the village worker is to serve the villagers, and he can best serve them if he keeps the eleven vows in front of him as a beacon-light. The vows are contained in two couplets com-posed by Vinoba and now repeated at each prayer by inmates of most of the Ashrams in the country:

आहिंसा सत्य अस्तेय ब्रह्मचर्य असंग्रह ।
शरीरश्रम अस्वाद सर्वत्र भयवर्जन ॥
सर्वधर्मी समानत्व स्वदेशी स्पर्शभावना ।
हीं एकादश सेवावीं नम्रत्वें व्रतनिश्चयें ॥

[Non-violence, truth, non-stealing, *brahma-charya*, non-possession, body-labour, control of the palate, fearlessness, equal respect for all religions, *swadeshi* (restricting oneself to the use and service of one's nearest surroundings in preference to those more remote), spirit of unexclusive brotherhood—these eleven vows should be observed in a spirit of humility.]

How is he to earn his livelihood? Is he to draw an allowance from an institution, or to earn it by labouring for it, or to depend upon the village for it? The ideal way is to depend upon the village. There is no shame therein, but humility. There is no scope for self-indulgence either, for I cannot think of a village which would encourage or tolerate self-indulgence. All that the worker need do is to work for the village all his working hours, and to collect whatever grain and vegetables he needed from the village. He may collect a little money too (for postage and other mone-tary expenditure) if he should need it, though

I do not think he could not do without it. The village would willingly support him if he has gone there at the invitation of the village. I can conceive an occasion when the villagers might not be able to tolerate his views and withdraw their support, as, for instance, they did when I admitted untouchables in the Satyagrahashram in 1915. Then he should work for his living. It is no use depending on an institution.

The village worker is in the village to do as much body labour as possible and to teach the villagers to outgrow idleness. He might do any kind of labour, but give preference to scavenging. Scavenging was certainly productive labour. I like some of the workers' insistence on devoting at least half an hour on work entirely of service and of a productive kind. Scavenging certainly came under that category. Also grinding; for, money saved is money gained.

I have no doubt that the village worker must be prepared to account for every minute of his waking hours and must fill them with work and mention it distinctly in his diary. A real diary is a mirror of the diarist's mind and soul, but many might find it difficult to make a truthful record of their mind's activities. In that case they may confine themselves to a record of their physical activities. But it should not be done in a haphazard way. Simply saying, "Worked in the kitchen" would not do. One may have whiled away one's time in the kitchen. Specific items of work should be mentioned.

Service of *dublas*, means readiness to share their toil and their hardships, and to get into touch with their masters and to see that they dealt with them justly and kindly.

The village worker will leave politics alone. He
may become a Congress member, but he may not take
part in an election campaign. He has his work cut out
for himself. The Village Industries Association and the
Spinners' Association were both created by the Congress, and yet they work independently of the Congress. That is why they and their members steer
clear of all Congress politics. That is the non-violent
way.

He will also leave village factions alone. He
must go and settle there determined to do without
most of the things he does not do without in a city.
If I sit down in a village I should have to decide what
things I should not take with me to the village, however inherently harmless those things may be. The
question is whether those things will sort well or ill
with the life of an ordinary villager. He will be incorruptible and stand like a rock against the inroad
of temptations and save the village from them. Even
one pure soul can save a whole village, as one
Bibhishana saved Lanka. Sodom and Gomorrah were
not destroyed so long as there was one pure soul left
in them. 9

II

[In answer to a question if a village worker can allow
himself milk, fruit and vegetables which villagers cannot
afford, Gandhiji wrote:]

The main thing to be borne in mind by the
village worker is that he is in the village for the villagers' service, and it is his right and his duty to
allow himself such articles of diet and other necessaries as would keep him fit and enable him to fulfil
his function. This will necessarily involve the acceptance of a higher standard of living by the village

worker, but I have an impression that the villagers do not grudge the worker these necessary things. The worker's conscience is the test. He must be self-restrained, he will eat nothing in order to indulge his palate, he will go in for no luxuries, and will fill all his waking hours with work of service. In spite of this, it is likely that a handful of people will cavil at his mode of life. We have to live that criticism down. The diet I have suggested is not quite un-obtainable in a village, with a certain amount of labour. Milk can generally be obtained, and there are numerous fruits, e.g. *ber*, *karamda*, *mhora* flower, which are easily available, but which we count of no value because they are so easily available. There are all kinds of leaves available which grow wild in our villages, which we do not use because of sheer ignorance or laziness (if not snobbery). I am myself using numerous varieties of these green leaves which I had never tried before, but which I find I should have used. It is quite possible to make a cow in a vil-lage pay for her upkeep and maintenance. I have not tried the experiment but I think it should be possible. I have also an impression that it is not im-possible for the villagers to obtain and live on the same articles of diet as the village workers and thus to adopt the same standard of life. *10*

III

Q. In almost all villages there are parties and factions. When we draft local help, whether we wish it or not, we become involved in local power politics. How can we steer clear of this difficulty? Should we try to by-pass both parties and carry on work with the help of outside workers? Our experience has been that such work becomes entirely contingent upon outside aid and crumbles down as soon as the latter is withdrawn. What should we do then to develop local initiative and foster local co-operation?

A. Alas for India that parties and factions are to be found in the villages as they are to be found in our cities. And when power politics enter our villages with less thought of the welfare of the villages and more of using them for increasing the parties' own power, this becomes a hindrance to the progress of the villagers rather than a help. I would say that whatever be the consequence, we must make use as much as possible of local help and if we are free from the taint of power politics, we are not likely to go wrong. Let us remember that the English-educated men and women from the cities have criminally neglected the villages of India which are the backbone of the country. The process of remembering our neglect will induce patience. I have never gone to a single village which is devoid of an honest worker. We fail to find him when we are not humble enough to recognize any merit in our villages. Of course, we are to steer clear of local politics and this we shall learn to do when we accept help from all parties and no parties, wherever it is really good. I would regard it as fatal for success to by-pass villagers. As I knew this very difficulty I have tried rigidly to observe the rule of one village, one worker, except that where he or she does not know Bengali, an interpreter's help has been given. I can only say that this system has so far answered the purpose. I must, therefore, discount your experience. I would further suggest that we have got into the vicious habit of coming to hasty conclusions. Before pronouncing such a sweeping condemnation as is implied in the sentence that 'work becomes entirely contingent upon outside aid and crumbles down as soon as the latter is withdrawn', I would go so far as to say that even a few years' experience of residence in a single village, trying to work through local workers, should not be regarded as conclusive proof that work could not be done through and by local workers. The contrary is obviously true. It now becomes unnecessary for me to examine the last sentence in detail. I can categorically say to the principal worker : ' If you have any outside help, get rid of it. Work singly, courageously, intelligently with all the local help you can get and, if you do not succeed, blame only yourself and no one else and nothing else. ' *11*

Conversation with Trainees

Q. Do the village folk come to see you?

A. They do, but not without fear, and perhaps even suspicion. These also are among the many shortcomings of villagers. We have to rid them of these.

Q. How?

A. By gently insinuating ourselves into their affections. We must disabuse them of the fear that we have gone there to coerce them, we must show them by our behaviour that there is no intention to coerce, nor any selfish motive. But this is all patient work. You cannot quickly convince them of your *bona fides*.

Q. Don't you think that only those who work without any remuneration or allowance can inspire confidence in them, i.e. those who accept nothing whether from any Association or from the village?

A. No. They do not even know who is and who is not working for remuneration. What does impress them is the way in which we live, our habits, our talks, even our gestures. There may be a few who suspect us of a desire to earn; we have to dispel their suspicion no doubt. And then do not run away with the feeling that he who accepts nothing from an Association or from the village is by any means an ideal servant. He is often a prey to self-righteousness which debases one.

Q. You teach us village crafts. Is that to give us a means of earning our livelihood or to enable us to teach the villagers? If it is for the latter object, how can we master a craft in the course of a year?

A. You are being taught the ordinary crafts, because unless you know the principles you will not be able to help people with suggestions. The most enterprising among you would certainly earn a living by following a craft. The things we teach here are such that you are likely to be able to bring to the villagers better knowledge of them. We have improved grinding stones and rice-husking stones and oil-presses. We are carrying on experiments in improving our tools and we have to take the improvements to them. Above all there is truth and honesty in business that we have to teach them. They adulterate, milk, they adulterate oil, they will adulterate truth for petty gain. It is not their fault, it is ours. We have so long ignored them and only exploited them, never taught them anything better. By close contact with them we can easily correct their ways. Long neglect and isolation has dulled their intellect and even moral sense. We have to brighten them up and revive them all along the line. *12*

Danger from Within

No movement or organization having vitality
dies from external attack. It dies of internal decay.
What is necessary is character above suspicion, ceaseless effort accompanied by ever increasing knowledge
of the technique of the work and a life of rigorous
simplicity. Workers without character, living far
above the ordinary life of villagers, and devoid of the
knowledge required of them for their work, can produce no impression on the villagers.

As I write these lines instances of those workers
who for want of character or simple living damaged
the cause and themselves recur to my mind. Happily
instances of positive misconduct are rare. But the
greatest hindrance to the progress of the work lies in
the inability of workers of quality to support themselves on the village scale. If every one of such workers puts on his work a price which village service
cannot sustain, ultimately these organizations must be
wound up. For the insistence of payments on the
city scale except in rare and temporary cases would
imply that the gulf between cities and villages is un-
bridgeable. The village movement is as much an
education of the city people as of the villagers. Workers drawn from cities have to develop village mentality and learn the art of living after the manner of
villagers. This does not mean that they have to
starve like the villagers. But it does mean that there
must be a radical change in the old style of life. While
the standard of living in the villages must be raised
the city standard has to undergo considerable revi-
sion, without the worker being required in any way to
adopt a mode of life that would impair his health. *13*

Our Villages

A young man who is trying to live in a village and earn his livelihood has sent me a pathetic letter. He does not know much English. I am therefore giving the letter below in an abridged form:

"Three years ago when I was 20 years old I came to this village life after spending 15 years in a town. My domestic circumstances did not allow me to have college education. The work you have taken up for village revival has encouraged me to pursue village life. I have some land. My village has a population of nearly 2,500. After close contact with this village I find the following among more than three-fourths of the people:

(1) Party feelings and quarrels.

(2) Jealousy.

(3) Illiteracy.

(4) Wickedness.

(5) Disunion.

(6) Carelessness.

(7) Lack of manners.

(8) Adherence to the old meaningless customs.

(9) Cruelty.

This is an out of the way place. No great man has ever visited such remote villages. The company of great ones is essential for advancement. So I am afraid to live in this village. Shall I leave this village? If not, what guidance will you give me?"

Though no doubt there is exaggeration in the picture drawn by the young correspondent, his statement may be generally accepted. The reason for the tragic state is not far to seek. Villages have suffered long from neglect by those who have had the benefit of education. They have chosen the city life.

The village movement is an attempt to establish healthy contact with the villages by inducing those who are fired with the spirit of service to settle in them and find self-expression in the service of villagers. The defects noticed by the correspondent are not inherent in village life. Those who have settled in villages in the spirit of service are not dismayed by the difficulties facing them. They knew before they went that they would have to contend against many difficulties including even sullenness on the part of villagers. Only those, therefore, who have faith in themselves and in their mission will serve the villagers and influence their lives. A true life lived amongst the people is in itself an object-lesson that must produce its own effect upon immediate surroundings. The difficulty with the young man is, perhaps, that he has gone to the village merely to earn a living without the spirit of service behind it. I admit that village life does not offer attractions to those who go there in search of money. Without the incentive of service village life would jar after the novelty has worn out. No young man having gone to a village may abandon the pursuit on the slightest contact with difficulty. Patient effort will show that villagers are not very different from city-dwellers and that they will respond to kindliness and attention. It is no doubt true that one does not have in the villages the opportunity of contact with the great ones of the land. With the growth of village mentality the leaders will find it necessary to tour in the villages and establish a living touch with them. Moreover the companionship of the great and the good is available to all through the works of saints like Chaitanya, Ramakrishna, Tulsidas, Kabir, Nanak,

Dadu, Tukaram, Tiruvalluvar, and others too numerous to mention though equally known and pious.
The difficulty is to get the mind tuned to the reception
of permanent values. If it is modern though: —
political, social, economical, scientific — that is meant,
it is possible to procure literature that will satisfy
curiosity. I admit, however, that one does not find
such as easily as one finds religious literature. Saints
wrote and spoke for the masses. The vogue for trans-
lating modern thought to the masses in an acceptable
manner has not yet quite set in. But it must come in
time. I would, therefore, advise young men like my
correspondent not to give in but persist in their effort
and by their presence make the village more livable
and lovable. That they will do by serving the villages
in a manner acceptable to the villagers. Everyone
can make a beginning by making the villages cleaner
by their own labour and removing illiteracy to the
extent of their ability. And if their lives are clean,
methodical and industrious, there is no doubt that
the infection will spread in the villages in which they
may be working. 14

Pilgrimage to Villages

Shri Sitaram Sastry has been organizing what
may be called pilgrimages of workers who convey the
message of village service among their surroundings.
I would suggest that the pilgrims should avoid all
travelling by rail, motor, or even village carts. If they
will adopt my advice, they will observe that their work
will be more effective and that the expenses will be
practically nil. No more than two or three should
form a party. I would expect villagers to house and
feed the parties. Small parties will be no tax on the
resources of villagers, as large ones are likely to be.

The work of the parties should be more in the nature of sanitary service, survey of village conditions and instruction of the villagers as to what they can do without much, if any, outlay of money to improve their health and economic conditions. 15

New Ways for Old?

Workers must not, without considerable experience, interfere with the old tools, old methods and old partners. They will be safe if they think of improvements, retaining intact the old existing background. They will find that it is true economy. 16

All-round Village Service

A Samagra Gramasevak must know everybody living in the village and render them such service as he can. That does not mean that the worker will be able to do everything single-handed. He will show them the way of helping themselves and procure for them such help and materials as they require. He will train up his own helpers. He will so win over the villagers that they will seek and follow his advice. Supposing I go and settle down in a village with a *ghani*, I won't be an ordinary *ghanchi* earning 15-20 rupees a month. I will be a Mahatma *ghanchi*. I have used the word ' Mahatma ' in fun but what I mean to say is that as a *ghanchi* I will become a model for the villagers to follow. I will be a *ghanchi* who knows the Gita and the Quran. I will be learned enough to teach their children. I may not be able to do so for lack of time. The villagers will come to me and ask me: " Please make arrangements for our children's education. " I will tell them: "I can find you a teacher but you will have to bear the expenses. " And they will be prepared to do so most willingly. I will teach them spinning and when they come and ask me for the services of a weaver, I will find them a weaver on the same terms as I found them a teacher. And the weaver will teach them how to weave their own cloth. I will inculcate in them the importance of hygiene and sanitation and when they come and ask me for a sweeper, I will tell them: " I will be your sweeper and I will train you all in the job. " This is my conception of Samagra Gramaseva. 17

CHAPTER 28

GOVERNMENT AND THE VILLAGES

What the Government Can Do

It is legitimate to ask what Congress Ministers will do for Khaddar and other village industries now that they are in office. Whether a Minister is separately appointed or not, a department for the work is surely necessary. In these times of scarcity of food and clothing, this department can render the greatest help. The Ministers have experts at their disposal through the A.I.S.A. and the A.I.V.I.A.It is possible to clothe today the whole of India in Khadi on the smallest outlay and in the shortest time possible. Each Provincial Government has to tell the villagers that they must manufacture their own Khaddar for their own use. This brings in automatic local production and distribution. And there will undoubtedly be a surplus for the cities at least to a certain extent which, in its turn, will reduce the pressure on the local mills. The latter will then be able to take part in supplying the want of cloth in other parts of the world.

How can this result be brought about?

The Governments should notify the villagers that they will be expected to manufacture Khaddar for the needs of their villages within a fixed date after which no cloth will be supplied to them. The Governments in their turn will supply the villagers with cotton seed or cotton wherever required, at cost price and the tools of manufacture also at cost, to be recovered in easy instalments payable, in, say, five years or more. They will supply them with instructors wherever necessary and undertake to buy surplus stock of Khaddar, provided that the villagers in question have their cloth requirements supplied from their own manufacture. This should do away with cloth shortage without fuss and with very little overhead charges.

The villages will be surveyed and a list prepared of things that can be manufactured locally with little or no help and which may be required for village use or for sale outside, such for instance, as *ghani*-pressed oil and cakes, burning oil prepared through *ghanis*, hand-pounded rice, *tadgud*, honey, toys, mats, handmade paper, village soap, etc. If enough care is thus taken the villages, most of them as good as dead or dying, will hum with life and exhibit the immense possibilities they have of supplying most of their wants themselves and of the cities and towns of India.

Then there is the limitless cattle wealth of India suffering from criminal neglect. Goseva Sangh, as yet not properly experienced, can still supply valuable aid.

Without the basic training the villagers are being starved for education. This desideratum can be supplied by the Hindustani Talimi Sangh. *1*

If I Were the Minister

My views, expressed above, remain unaltered.
One thing has created a misunderstanding. Some
friends have read compulsion in that note. I am
sorry for the obscurity. In it I had answered the
question as to what representative governments could
do if they wished. I had, I hope pardonably, assumed
that such government's notices too could not be inter-
preted as compulsion. For every act of a bona fide
representative government would assume consent
of the voters represented. The voters would mean the
whole populace, whether registered as voters or not.
With the background, I wrote that the government
should notify to the villagers that mill cloth would
not be supplied to the villagers after a certain fixed
date, so as to enable them to wear Khadi prepared by
themselves.

Whatever the meaning of my above article of 28th
April last, I want to state that any scheme adopted
about Khadi, without the willing co-operation of those
concerned must mean death to Khadi as a means
for attaining Swaraj. Then the taunt that Khadi
was a return to the darkness and slavery of the Middle
Ages would be true. But I have held the contrary
view. Whilst Khadi under compulsion was a badge
of slavery, Khadi intelligently and voluntarily prepared, primarily for one's own use, was easily the
badge of our freedom. Freedom is nothing if it is
not all-round self-help. I, for one, would have nothing
to do with Khadi, if it were not a free man's privilege
as well as duty.

A friendly critic asks whether Khadi thus prepared could also and at the same time be for sale. Yes,
if sale is its secondary use; not if manufacture for sale

is its only or even primary use. That we began with sale of Khadi shows temporary necessity as well as our limited vision. Experience is a great teacher. It has taught us many things. Not the least is its primary use. But it is by no means the last. But I must leave this fascinating field of speculation and proceed definitely to answer the question put in the heading.

My first business as the Minister in charge of revival of the villages as the centre of all governmental activity, would be to find out from among the Permanent Service honest and incorruptible men capable for the work. I would put the best among them in touch with the A.I.S.A. and the A.I.V.I.A., creations of the Congress, and bring in a scheme for giving the village-crafts the greatest encouragement. I would stipulate, there should be no compulsion on the villagers, that they must not slave for others and that they should be taught to help themselves and rely upon their own labour and skill for the production of articles of food, cloth and other necessaries. The scheme would thus have to be comprehensive. I would instruct my first man, therefore, to see the Hindustani Talimi Sangh and see what it has to say.

Let me assume that the scheme, thus produced, contains a clause, saying that the villagers themselves declare that they would not want mill cloth, say, after one year from a fixed date, that they require cotton, wool and necessary implements and instruction, not as a gift but to be paid for on the easiest terms. The scheme provides too, that it will not apply at once to the whole of any province but only to a part to begin with. The scheme further tells one that the A.I.S.A. will guide and assist the working of the scheme.

Being convinced of its soundness, I would give it legal form in consultation with the law department and issue a notification, fully describing the genesis of the scheme. The villagers as well as the mill-owners and others would have been party to it. The notification will show clearly that it is the people's measure, though bearing the Government stamp. The Government money will be used for the benefit of the poorest villagers, making the largest return possible to the people concerned. It will, therefore, be probably the most profitable investment in which expert assistance will be voluntary and overhead charges the least item. The notification will give in detail, the whole cost to the country and the return to the people.

The only question for me as Minister is whether A.I.S.A. has the conviction and capacity to shoulder the burden of creating and guiding a Khadi scheme to success. If it has, I would put my little barque to sea with all confidence. 2

CHAPTER 29

INDIA AND THE WORLD

When India becomes self-supporting, self-reliant, and proof against temptations and exploitation, she will cease to be the object of greedy attraction for any power in the West or the East, and will then feel secure without having to carry the burden of expensive armament. Her internal economy will be India's strongest bulwark against aggression. *1*

My notion of *Purna Swaraj* is not isolated independence but healthy and dignified independence. My nationalism, fierce though it is, is not exclusive, is not devised to harm any nation or individual. Legal maxims are not so legal as they are moral. I believe in the eternal truth of *sic utere tuo ut alienum non laedas* (use thy own property so as not to injure thy neighbour's). *2*

A free democratic India will gladly associate herself with other free nations for mutual defence against aggression and for economic co-operation. She will work for the establishment of a real world order based on freedom and democracy, utilizing the world's knowledge and resources for the progress and advancement of humanity. *3*

It only means that the Western nations have to use their skill. If they want to use their skill abroad, from philanthropic motives, America would say, 'Well, we know how to make bridges, we won't keep it a secret, but we say to the whole world, we will teach you how to make bridges and we will charge you nothing.' America says, 'Where other nations can grow one blade of wheat, we can grow two thousand. ' Then, America should teach that art free of charge to those who will learn it, but not aspire to grow wheat for the whole world, which would spell a sorry day for the world indeed. *4*

[Africans wanted to know what India could give them and how they could achieve co-operative industrialization in order to be saved from the terrible exploitation under which they were suffering.]

The commerce between India and Africa, will be of ideas and services, not of manufactured goods against raw materials after the fashion of Western exploiters. Then, India can offer you the spinning wheel. If I had discovered it when

I was in South Africa, I would have introduced it among the Africans who were my neighbours in Phoenix. You can grow cotton, you have ample leisure and plenty of manual skill. You should study and adopt the lesson of the village crafts we are trying to revive. Therein lies the key to your salvation. 5

' Has the spinning wheel a message for America ? Can it serve as a counter weapon to the atom bomb ? '

I do feel that it has a message for the U.S.A. and the whole world. . . . I have not the slightest doubt that the saving of India and of the world lies in the wheel. If India becomes the slave of the machine, then, I say, Heaven save the world. 6

I feel in the innermost recesses of my heart . . . that the world is sick unto death of blood-spilling. The world is seeking a way out, and I flatter myself with the belief that perhaps it will be the privilege of the ancient land of India to show that way out to the hungering world. 7

If India fails, Asia dies. It has been aptly called the nursery of many blended cultures and civilizations. Let India be and remain the hope of all the exploited races of the earth, whether in Asia, Africa or in any part of the world. 8

We do not want to cut adrift from the whole world. We will have a free interchange with all nations, but the present forced interchange has to go. We do not want to be exploited, neither do we want to exploit any other nation. Through the scheme we look forward to making all children producers, and so to change the face of the whole nation, for it will permeate the whole of our social being. But that does not mean that we cut adrift from the whole world. There will be nations that will want to interchange with others because they cannot produce certain things. They will certainly depend on other nations for them, but the nations that will provide for them should not exploit them.

'But if you simplify your life to such an extent that you need nothing from other countries, you will isolate yourselves from them; whereas I want you to be responsible for America also.'

It is by ceasing to exploit and to be exploited that we can be responsible for America. For America will then follow our example and there will be no difficulty in a free interchange between us. *9*

I know that the work (of shaping the ideal village) is as difficult as to make of India an ideal country. . . . But if one can produce one ideal village, he will have provided a pattern not only for the whole country but perhaps for the whole world. More than this a seeker may not aspire after. *10*

'In free India whose interest shall be supreme? If a neighbouring State is in want, would India adopt an attitude of isolationism, saying that her own needs must come first?'

A truly independent and free India would rush to the help of her neighbours in distress. A man whose spirit of sacrifice does not go beyond his own community, himself becomes, and makes his community, selfish. The logical sequel of self-sacrifice is that the individual sacrifices himself for the community, the community for the district, the district for the Province, the Province for the nation, and the nation for the world. A drop from the ocean perishes without doing any good. As a part of the ocean, it shares the glory of carrying on its bosom whole fleets of mighty ships. *11*

Let no. one commit the mistake of thinking, that Rama-rajya means a rule of the Hindus. My Rama is another name for Khuda or God. I want *Khudai Raj,* which is the same thing as the Kingdom of God on Earth. The establishment of such a Rajya would not only mean welfare of the whole of the Indian people but of the whole world. *12*

I would like to see India free and strong so that she may offer herself as a willing and pure sacrifice for the betterment of the world. The individual, being pure, sacrifices himself for the family, the latter for the village, the village for the district, the district for the province, the province for the nation, the nation for all. *13*

Through Swaraj we would serve the whole world. *14*

There is no limit to extending our service to our neighbours across our State-made frontiers. God never made those frontiers. *15*

SOURCES

[Note: *H.* stands for *Harijan, Y. I.* for *Young India* and *Natesan* for *Speeches and Writings of Mahatma Gandhi*, 4th ed. Natesan, Madras.]

Chapter 1

1 *Y. I.*, 19-3-'31, p. 38
2 *Y. I.*, 15-10-'31, p. 305
3 *Y. I.*, 29-1-'25, pp. 40-41
4 *H.*, 2-1-'37, p. 374
5 *Y. I.*, 1-12-'27, pp.402-03
6 *Y. I.*, 6-8-'25, p. 276
7 *Y. I.*, 26-6-'24, p. 210
8 *Y. I.*, 28-7-'21, p. 238
9 *Y. I.*, 1-5-'30, p. 149
10 *Y. I.*, 16-4-'31, p. 78
11 *Y. I.*, 23-1-'30, p. 26
12 *Y. I.*, 5-3-'31, p. 1
13 *Y. I.*, 5-3-'31, p. 1
14 *Y. I.*, 26-3-'31, pp. 46-47
15 *Y. I.*, 26-3-'31, p. 51
16 *Constructive Programme*, 1961, p. 7
17 *Y. I.*, 18-6-'31, p. 147
18 *H.*, 2-1-'37, p. 374
19 *H.*, 27-5-'39, p. 143
20 *H.*, 25-3-'39, p. 64
21 *H.*, 25-3-'39, p. 65

Chapter 2

1 *Mahatma Gandhi—The Last Phase*, 1956, Vol. I, pp. 190-91
2 *Mahatma Gandhi—The Last Phase*, 1956, Vol. I, pp. 539-40
3 *H.*, 18-1-'48, p. 526

Chapter 3

1 *Y. I.*, 12-11-'31, p. 355
2 *Y. I.*, 22-10-'31, p. 318
3 *Y. I.*, 7-10-'26, p. 348
4 *Y. I.*, 25-7-'29, p. 244
5 *Y. I.*, 7-10-'26, p. 348
6 *Y. I.*, 17-3-'27, p. 85
7 *H.*, 29-8-'36, p. 226
8 *H.*, 1-9-'46, p. 285
9 *Y. I.*, 30-4-'31, p. 88
10 *Natesan*, pp. 353-54
11 *H.*, 29-9-'40, p. 299
12 *H.*, 28-1-'39, p. 438
13 *H.*, 20-12-'28, p. 422
14 *Y. I.*, 7-10-'26, p. 348
15 *Y. I.*, 20-11-'24, p. 386
16 *Y. I.*, 5-11-'25, p. 377
17 *Y. I.*, 15-4-'26, p. 142
18 *Y. I.*, 3-11-'21, p. 350
19 *Y. I.*, 17-6-'26, p. 218

20   *Y. I.*, 13-11-'24, p. 378
21   *H.*, 27-2-'37, p. 18
22   *H.*, 2-11-'34, pp. 301-02
23   *Towards New Horizons*, 1959, pp. 45-46

Chapter 4

1   *Hindustan Standard*, 6-12-'44
2   *Amrita Bazar Patrika*, 30-6-'44
3   *Hind Swaraj*, 1962, p. 94
4   *H.*, 31-3-'46, p. 63
5   *Y. I.*, 17-3-'27, p. 86
6   *Gleanings*, 1949, p. 17
7   *H.*, 23-6-'46, p. 198
8   *H.*, 25-8-'46, p. 282
9   *H.*, 4-4-'36, p. 63
10   *H.*, 4-4-'36, pp. 63-64
11   *Natesan.* p. 323
12   *Y. I.*, 30-4-'31, p. 94
13   *H.*, 1-3-'35, p. 21
14   *Y. I.*, 11-9-'24, p. 300
15   *H.*, 1-3-'35, p. 21
16   *H.*, 1-3-'35, p. 21
17   *H.*, 7-3-'36, p. 30
18   *H.*, 11-4-'36, p. 68
19   *H.*, 16-5-'36, p. 112
20   *H.*, 27-2-'37, p. 18
21   *H.*, 9-10-'37, p. 293
22   *Y. I.*, 9-11-'29, p. 364

Chapter 5

1   *Y. I.*, 26-12-'29, p. 420
2   *H.*, 29-8-'36, p. 226

3   *H.*, 20-1-'40, p. 423
4   *Bunch of Old Letters*, 1958, pp. 506-7 (5-10-'45)
5   *H.*, 26-7-'42, p. 238
6   *H.*, 9-1-'37, p. 383
7   *Bunch of Old Letters*, 1958, pp. 506-07 (5-10-'45)

Chapter 6

1   *Y. I.*, 13-11-'24, p. 378
2   *H.*, 18-1-'42, p. 5
3   *Y. I.*, 15-11-'28, p. 381
4   *Y. I.*, 26-12-'24, p. 421
5   *Natesan*, p. 350
6   *Natesan*, p. 350
7   *H.*, 23-3-'47, p. 79
8   *Y. I.*, 6-10-'21, p. 314
9   *Y. I.*, 26-3-'31, p. 49
10   *From Yeravda Mandir*, 1957, p. 34
11   *H.*, 29-6-'35, p. 156
12   *Y. I.*, 13-10-'21, p. 326
13   *H.*, 29-6-'35, p. 156
14   *H.*, 23-2-'47, p. 36
15   *Y. I.*, 13-10-'21, p. 325
16   *H.*, 9-10-'37, p. 292
17   *H.*, 15-1-'38, p. 416
18   *Y. I.*, 17-3-'27, p. 86
19   *Constructive Programme*, 1961, p. 18
20   *H.*, 25-8-'40, p. 260
21   *H.*, 30-12-'39, p. 391
22   *H.*, 4-11-'39, p. 331
23   *Natesan*, pp. 336-42

24 *From Yeravda Mandir*, 1957, Chap. XVI, pp. 64-67
25 *Towards New Horizons*, 1959, p. 8
26 *H.*, 26-7-'42, p. 238
27 *H.*, 27-7-'35, p. 188
28 *H.*, 28-7-'46, p. 236
29 *H.*, 26-7-'42, p. 238
30 *H.*, 9-3-'47, pp. 58-59
31 *H.*, 26-7-'42, p. 238
32 *H.*, 28-7-'46, p. 236
33 *H.*, 26-7-'42, p. 238
34 *H.*, 26-7-'42, p. 238
35 *Towards New Horizons*, p. 194
36 *H.*, 31-7-'37, p. 197

Chapter 7

1 *Y. I.*, 11-4-'29, pp. 114-15
2 *From Yeravda Mandir*, 1957, Chap. IX, pp. 35-37
3 *Y. I.*, 8-1-'25, pp. 15-16
4 *Y. I.*, 26-3-'31, p. 49
5 *H.*, 29-6-'35, p. 156
6 *H.*, 1-6-'35, p. 125
7 *H.*, 29-6-'35, p. 156
8 *Y. I.*, 13-8-'25, p. 282
9 *H.*, 11-5-'35, p. 99

Chapter 8

1 *Y. I.*, 26-11-'31, p. 368
2 *H.*, 25-8-'40, p. 260
3 *Y. I.*, 5-11-'31, p. 384
4 *H.*, 13-7-'40, p. 205

5 *H.*, 16-3-'47, p. 67

Chapter 9

1 *H.*, 3-6-'39, p. 145
2 *Modern Review*, 1935, p. 412
3 *H.*, 3-12-'38, p. 358
4 *H.*, 7-1-'39, p. 417
5 *H.*, 16-12-'39, p. 376
6 *H.*, 22-2-'42, p. 49

Chapter 10

1 *Natesan*, pp. 336-44
2 *From Yeravda Mandir*, 1957, Chap. XVI, p. 66

Chapter 11

1 *The Ideology of the Charkha*, 1951, pp. 86-88
2 *H.*, 30-11-'35, p. 333
3 *Khadi—Why and How*, 1959, p. 166
4 *H.*, 19-10-'47, p. 379
5 *H.*, 5-4-'42, p. 107
6 *H.*, 27-7-'35, p. 188
7 *H.*, 22-8-'36, p. 217
8 *Khadi—Why and How*, 1959, p. 162
9 *H.*, 20-4-'35, p. 80
10 *Y. I.*, 25-4-'29, p. 135
11 *Y. I.*, 10-6-'26, p. 214
12 *H.*, 6-10-'46, p. 344

Chapter 12

1 *Y. I.*, 28-5-'31, p. 123

2 *H.*, 28-7-'46, p. 236

3 *H.*, 18-1-'48, p. 517

4 *H.*, 4-1-'48, pp. 499-500

Chapter 13

1 *H.*, 21-12-'47, pp. 480

2 *H.*, 8-5-'37, p. 104

3 *H.*, 5-6-'37, p. 130

4 *H.*, 5-6-'37, p. 131

5 *H.*, 28-8-'37, p. 225

6 *H.*, 2-10-'37, p. 282

7 *H.*, 31-7-'37, p. 197

8 *H.*, 11-9-'37, p. 256

9 *H.*, 18-9-'37, p. 261

10 *H.*, 18-9-'37, p. 42

11 *H.*, 9-10-'37, p. 292

12 *H.*, 9-10-'37, p. 293

13 *H.*, 11-6-'38, p. 143

14 *H.*, 2-11-'47, p. 393

15 *H.*, 18-2-'39, pp. 14-15

16 *Constructive Programme*, 1961, p. 18

Chapter 14

1 *Khadi—Why and How*, 1959, p. 162

2 *Khadi—Why and How*, 1959, p. 181

3 *From Yeravda Mandir*, 1957, pp. 35-37

4 *H.*, 25-8-'46, pp. 281-82

5 *H.*, 28-1-'39, p. 439

6 *H.*, 28-1-'39, p. 439

7 *H.*, 1-3-'35, p. 21

8 *H.*, 16-5-'36, p. 111

9 *H.*, 6-3-'37, p. 29

10 *H.*, 6-3-'37, p. 29

11 *The Bombay Chronicle*, 28-10-'44

12 *H.*, 8-2-'48, p. 21

Chapter 15

1 *The Bombay Chronicle*, 28-10-'44

2 *H.*, 2-1-'37, p. 375

3 *H.*, 20-5-'39, p. 133

4 *H.*, 20-4-'40, p. 97

5 *Amrita Bazar Patrika*, 2-8-'34

6 *Amrita Bazar Patrika*, 3-8-'34

7 *Amrita Bazar Patrika*, 2-8-'34

8 *Amrita Bazar Patrika*, 2-8-'34

9 *H.*, 5-12-'36, p. 338

10 *Y. I.*, 5-12-'29 p. 396

11 *Y. I.*, 28-5-'31, p. 120

12 *H.*, 4-5-'47, p. 134

13 *H.*, 1-6-'47, p. 172

14 *H.*, 2-1-'37, p. 375

15 *H.*, 9-3-'47, p. 58

Chapter 16

1 *H.*, 15-2-'42, p. 39

2 *H.*, 9-3-'47, p. 59

3 *H.*, 9-3-'47, p. 59

Chapter 17

1   *H.*, 28-12-'47, p. 484
2   *H.*, 28-12-'47, p. 488
3   *H.*, 1-3-'35, p. 20
4   *H.*, 15-3-'35, p. 36
5   *H.*, 17-8-'35, pp. 213-15
6   *H.*, 24-8-'35, pp. 218-19, 224
7   *H.*, 26-7-'42, p. 238

Chapter 18

1   *H.*, 19-10-'47, pp. 376-77
2   *H.*, 25-1-'42, p. 12
3   *H.*, 24-2-'46, p. 19
4   *Y. I.*, 2-4-'25 p. 118 & *H.*, 14-9-'35, p. 244

Chapter 19

1   *Constructive Programme*, 1951, pp. 11-14
2   *Y. I.*, 17-9-'25, p. 321
3   *H.*, 17-11-'46, p. 404
4   *Y. I.*, 20-10-'21, p. 329
5   *Y. I.*, 21-7-'20, p. 4
6   *Y. I.*, 3-11-'21, p. 350
7   *Y. I.*, 8-12-'21, p. 405
8   *Y. I.*, 21-8-'24, p. 277
9   *Y. I.*, 18-6-'25, p. 211
10 *Y. I.*, 27-8-'25, p. 299
11 *Y. I.*, 17-2-'27, p. 52
12 *H.*, 27-4-'34, p. 85
13 *Y. I.*, 27-5-'26, p. 190
14 *Y. I.*, 27-5-'26, p. 190
15 *Y. I.*, 30-9-'26, p. 341
16 *H.*, 13-4-'40, p. 85
17 *Y. I.*, 8-12-'21, p. 406

18 *Y. I.*, 29-6-'21, p. 206
19 *Y. I.*, 21-5-'25, p. 177
20 *Swaraj through Charkha*, 1945, p. 8
21 *Swaraj through Charkha*, 1945, p. 5
22 *Khadi—Why and How*, 1959, pp. 153-57
23 *Ideology of the Charkha*, 1959, p. 94
24 *Khadi—Why and How*, 1959, p. 149
25 *Khadi—Why and How*, 1959, p. 150
26 *Khadi—Why and How*, 1959, p. 151
27 *Khadi—Why and How*, 1959, p. 154
28 *Khadi—Why and How*, 1959, p. 181
29 *Khadi—Why and How*, 1959, p. 184
30 *Khadi—Why and How*, 1959, p. 185
31 *Khadi—Why and How*, 1959, p. 189
32 *H.*, 22-9-'46, p. 320
33 *H.*, 22-9-'46, p. 322
34 *H.*, 22-9-'46, p. 322

Chapter 20

1   *Cent Per Cent Swadeshi* 1958, p. 4
2   *Cent Per Cent Swadeshi*, 1958, p. 5

3   *H.*, 10-8-'34, p. 204
4   *H.*, 28-9-'34, p. 259
5   *H.*, 30-11-'34, p. 332
6   *H.*, 16-11-'34, p. 316
7   *H.*, 16-11-'34, p. 316
8   *H.*, 16-11-'34, p. 316
9   *H.*, 16-11-'34, p. 316
10 *H.*, 16-11-'34, p. 316
11 *H.*, 16-11-'34, p. 316
12 *H.*, 16-11-'34, p. 317
13 *H.*, 7-12-'34, p. 340
14 *H.*, 7-12-'34, pp. 340-41
15 *H.*, 7-12-'34, p. 341
16 *Constructive   Programme*,
    1961, pp. 16-17
17 *H.*, 4-1-'35, p. 372
18 *Khadi—Why   and   How*,
    1959, p. 150
19 *Khadi—Why   and   How*,
    1959, p. 151
20 *Khadi—Why   and   How*,
    1959, p. 159
21 *Khadi—Why   and   How*,
    1959, p. 162
22 *Khadi—Why   and   How*,
    1959, p. 163
23 *Khadi—Why   and   How*,
    1959, p. 177
24 *Khadi—Why   and   How*,
    1959, p. 181
25 *H.*, 25-1-'35, p. 400
26 *Y. I.*, 6-10-'21, p. 318
27 *Y. I.*, 22-10-'25, p. 361
28 *Y. I.*, 3-11-'27, p. 367

29 *H.*, 26-10-'34, p. 292
30 *H.*, 10-3-'46, p. 34
31 *H.*, 2-9-'39, p. 253
32 *Cent Per Cent Swadeshi*,
    1958 p. 5
33 *Key   to   Health*,   1960,
    pp. 33-34
34 *H.*, 1-2-'35, p. 407
35 *H.*, 7-9-'34, pp. 236-37
36 *Khadi—Why   and   How*,
    1959, p. 185
37 *H.*, 14-9-'34, p. 234
38 *H.*, 14-9-'34, p. 241
39 *Gram Udyog Patrika*, July
    1946

Chapter 21

1   *H.*, 3-7-'37, p. 168
2   *H.*, 16-9-'39, p. 276
3   *H.*, 15-9-'40, p. 282

Chapter 22

1   *H.*, 2-11-'34, p. 302
2   *Natesan*, p. 336
3   *Swaraj through Charkha*,
    1945, p. 5
4   *H.*, 2-2-'34, pp. 2, 6
5   *Khadi—Why   and   How*,
    1959, p. 166
6   *H.*, 7-7-'46, p. 209
7   *H.*, 18-1-'42, p. 5
8   *H.*, 25-3-'39, p. 65

Chapter 23

1   *Constructive   Programme*,
    1961, p. 15

2   *H.*, 8-2-'35, p. 416

Chapter 24

1   *Constructive   Programme,*
    1961, p. 21
2   *Key   to   Health,*   1960,
    p. 3
3   *Constructive   Programme,*
    1961, p. 22
4   *H.*, 7-4-'46, p. 69
5   *H.*, 26-5-'46, p. 153
6   *H.*, 2-6-'46, p. 165
7   *H.*, 11-8-'46, p. 257
8   *H.*, 11-8-'46, p. 260
9   *Key to Health,* 1960, p. 57
10 *Key to Health,* 1960,
    pp. 58-59
11 *Key to Health,* 1960, p. 59
12 *Key to Health,* 1960,
    pp. 59-60
13 *Key to Health,* 1960, p. 60
14 *Key to Health,* 1960, p. 61
15 *Key to Health,* 1960, p. 61
16 *Key to Health,* 1960, p. 62
17 *Key   to   Health,*   1960,
    pp. 63-65
18 *Key   to   Health,*   1960,
    pp. 67-69
19 *Key   to   Health,*   1960,
    pp. 71-72
20 *Key   to   Health,*   1960,
    pp. 73-75
21 *Key to Health,* 1960, p. 75
22 *Key to Health,* 1960, p. 76
23 *Key to Health,* 1960, p. 77

24 *Key to Health,* 1960, p. 78
25 *Key   to   Health,*   1960,
    pp. 79-81
26 *Key   to   Health,*   1960,
    pp. 81-82
27 *Key to Health,* 1960, p. 82
28 *Key to Health,* 1960, p. 82
29 *Key to Health,* 1960, p. 83
30 *H.*, 5-4-'35, p. 59
31 *H.*, 11-5-'35, p. 100
32 *H.*, 9-11-'35, p. 308

Chapter 25

1   *Key   to   Health,*   1960,
    pp. 13-27

Chapter 26

1   *H.*, 18-6-'38, p. 152
2   *H.*, 1-9-'40, p. 265
3   *H.*, 5-5-'46, p. 113

Chapter 27

1   *H.*, 23-5-'36, p. 119
2   *H.*, 25-3-'39, p. 64
3   *H.*, 15-2-'48, p. 32
4   *H.*, 31-8-'34, pp. 227-30
5   *H.*, 9-1-'37, p. 383
6   *H.*, 18-8-'40, p. 252
7   *H.*, 2-11-'35, p. 302
8   *H.*, 23-11-'35, pp. 324-25
9   *H.*, 29-2-'36, pp. 18-19
10 *H.*, 24-8-'35, p. 223
11 *H.*, 2-3-'47, p. 44
12 *H.*, 25-7-'36, p. 187
13 *H.*, 11-4-'36, p. 68
14 *H.*, 20-2-'37, p. 16

15   *H.*, 22-3-'35, p. 42

16   *H.*, 29-3-'35, p. 49

17   *H.*, 17-3-'46, p. 42

Chapter 28

1   *H.*, 28-4-'46, p. 104

2   *H.*, 1-9-'46, p. 288

Chapter 29

1   *Y. I.*, 2-7-'31, p. 161

2   *Y. I.*, 26-3-'31, p. 51

3   *H.*, 23-9-'39, p. 278

4   *H.*, 2-11-'34, p. 302

5   *H.*, 24-2-'46, p. 18

6   *H.*, 17-11-'46, p. 404

7   *India's Case for Swaraj,* 1932, p. 209

8   *H.*, 5-10-'47, p. 354

9   *H.*, 12-2-'38, p. 2

10   *Towards New Horizons,* 1959, p. 99

11   *Towards New Horizons,* 1959, p. 200

12   *Towards New Horizons,* 1959, p. 200

13   *Y. I.*, 17-9-'25, p. 321

14   *Y. I.*, 16-4-'31, p. 79

15   *Y. I.*, 31-12-'31, p 427

INDEX